THE
SOCIOLOGY
OF EARLY
CHILDHOOD

CRITICAL PERSPECTIVES

Sara Miller McCune founded SAGE Publishing in 1965 to support the dissemination of usable knowledge and educate a global community. SAGE publishes more than 1000 journals and over 800 new books each year, spanning a wide range of subject areas. Our growing selection of library products includes archives, data, case studies and video. SAGE remains majority owned by our founder and after her lifetime will become owned by a charitable trust that secures the company's continued independence.

Los Angeles | London | New Delhi | Singapore | Washington DC | Melbourne

THE SOCIOLOGY OF EARLY CHILDHOOD

CRITICAL PERSPECTIVES

NORMAN GABRIEL

Los Angeles | London | New Delhi
Singapore | Washington DC | Melbourne

Los Angeles | London | New Delhi
Singapore | Washington DC | Melbourne

SAGE Publications Ltd
1 Oliver's Yard
55 City Road
London EC1Y 1SP

SAGE Publications Inc.
2455 Teller Road
Thousand Oaks, California 91320

SAGE Publications India Pvt Ltd
B 1/I 1 Mohan Cooperative Industrial Area
Mathura Road
New Delhi 110 044

SAGE Publications Asia-Pacific Pte Ltd
3 Church Street
#10-04 Samsung Hub
Singapore 049483

Editor: Natalie Aguilera
Assistant editor: Delayna Spencer
Production editor: Katherine Haw
Copyeditor: Rosemary Campbell
Proofreader: Rebecca Storr
Indexer: Elizabeth Ball
Marketing manager: Sally Ransom
Cover design: Tristan Tutak
Typeset by: C&M Digitals (P) Ltd, Chennai, India
Printed by CPI Group (UK) Ltd, Croydon, CR0 4YY

© Norman Gabriel 2017

First published 2017

Library of Congress Control Number: 2016952261

British Library Cataloguing in Publication data

A catalogue record for this book is available from the British Library

ISBN 978-1-4462-7298-5
ISBN 978-1-4462-7299-2 (pbk)

At SAGE we take sustainability seriously. Most of our products are printed in the UK using FSC papers and boards. When we print overseas we ensure sustainable papers are used as measured by the PREPS grading system. We undertake an annual audit to monitor our sustainability.

CONTENTS

ABOUT THE AUTHOR

Norman Gabriel is a sociologist teaching Early Childhood Studies at Plymouth University. Inspired by Norbert Elias, his research interests are in relational sociology and the sociology of early childhood. With Professor Stephen Mennell he co-edited, *Norbert Elias and Figurational Research: Processual Thinking in Sociology* (2011), a monograph for The Sociological Review series. He is currently working on a book on Norbert Elias's political sociology (co-authored with Professor Lars Bo Kaspersen).

ACKNOWLEDGEMENTS

This book is the culmination of a number of years of teaching and researching in Early Childhood Studies. The initial idea came from a conversation with Jenny Willan, a former colleague who suggested that there was a 'gap' in the sociological literature exploring the lives of young children. Many thanks to Chris Rojek who encouraged me to develop a proposal that would focus on the sociology of early childhood.

I would like to take this opportunity to thank Stephen Mennell for his continuous and generous support - his introductory book to Norbert Elias inspired me. I hope readers will become aware of the deep gratitude I owe to Elias's radical sociological thinking and its application to early childhood. My good friend Lars Bo Kaspersen also gave me excellent advice and wise counsel when I most needed it – a big thank you for all the great times in Copenhagen.

Thanks to Gina my beautiful love for keeping me on firm foundations during the writing process and to our two wonderful sons, Joseph, for your strong commitment and dedication to keeping alive our traditions and Jacob, long may you continue to challenge me in our discussions. And to Mum and Dad for bringing me up with deep trust and security – may their memory always be a source of inspiration for future generations.

1

INTRODUCTION

Introduction

In this book we will develop a relational sociology of early childhood by focusing on the earliest experiences of young children. At birth, babies are born in total dependency on their mother or carers and only gradually do they develop attachments to other people around them - fathers, siblings, grandparents, other relatives and friends, teachers or classmates. Young children are born into and grow up in interdependent relationships that change but are historically structured in different societies. In early childhood, this network is relatively small and the balance is tilted towards dependency on older adults. The lives of young children should therefore be seen as intersections in a network that slowly form part of a wider figuration of relationships in society.

As they grow up they look forward to becoming adults, making connections across generations. When he was seven years of age my younger son Jacob made a subtle distinction about his Grandad, my father-in-law, and my Dad, his Grandpa, 'Granddad, you're old but grandpa is an antique'. Later as adults we look back at our youngest years, trying to establish some formative influences in our earliest experiences. Richard Feynman (1988: 16), one of the most important physicists of the twentieth century, talked about the wonderful influence of his father, the way he encouraged him to explore some of the deep connections behind the principles of science:

> I've been caught, so to speak – like someone who was given something wonderful when he was a child, and he's always looking for it again. I'm always looking, like a child, for the wonders I'm going to find – maybe not every time, but every once in a while.

This chapter will introduce you to why the study of young children has become such an important area for investigation, discussing some of the key theoretical concepts that can be used to understand their early lives in contemporary society. I will mainly focus on the experiences of young children growing up in the United Kingdom today, though relevant comparisons will be made with young children in other countries to emphasise some of the universal features that are common to their experiences and development.

Early Childhood

Early childhood is a complex field with many varied terms, including early years, early childhood development, early care, early care and education, and early childhood education and care. While there are no clear definitions, the terms 'early childhood' and 'early years' are among the two most popular internationally and are often used interchangeably by researchers. Therefore, the two terms 'early childhood' and 'early years' will be used in this book. There is also some controversy regarding the age span of children that should be included in early childhood, with most using the term to refer to young children from birth to age eight. Despite the contested nature of the ages to be included in early childhood, the vast majority of international researchers consider early childhood or the early years as embracing birth to age eight years (Farrell et al., 2015).

The early years sector in the UK can be characterised as a mixed economy of provision marked by variation in quality, poor qualification levels, low pay and low status. This low status of the early childhood worker, rooted in the relationship between 'childcare' and 'mothering', can easily become relegated to 'women's work'. As a highly gendered employment sector strongly connected with the affective realms of caring and nurturance, women who work in this sector have been perceived to lack professionalism (see Dahlberg et al., 1999).

Osgood (2010) argues that tensions over what it means to be an early years professional are made even more complex because nursery workers need to practise a high degree of emotional labour, working collegially and managing the emotions and expectations of parents. Emotional investment is a necessary and integral part of early years practice because the work involves strong feelings towards young children and their families, as well as supporting and caring for colleagues and maintaining a relationship with the wider community (Dahlberg and Moss, 2005). She argues that the emotions are a vital aspect of practice that should be built upon to support future professional development in the early years workforce.

Sociology of Early Childhood

One of the key arguments in this book is that in order to develop a distinctive sociology of early childhood, one should not only focus on the relational aspects of early childhood and adulthood, but at the same time view them as long-term processes with deep historical roots. My emphasis on a relational approach to young children and their relationships is based on a relational turn in sociology (see Dépelteau and Powell, 2013), one which views the social as dynamic, continuous and processual. In Chapter 2, I will explain how these social processes should be seen as dynamic and structured - although transitions occur in dramatic spurts, the history of childhood does not proceed in discrete stages. Short-term changes must be both distinguished from and connected to transformations on a larger scale and to underlying developments in the long run.

To understand these different levels of complexity, De Swaan (1990) offers a very useful metaphor of a clock with wheels which turn at different speeds. Some cogs, moving so slowly that the observer hardly notices any movement, drive other faster wheels that finally connect to a balance wheel, which by its frenetic oscillation controls the movement of the entire machine. Within the very slow clock of biological time the wheels of human history turn, and within this, the much faster cogs of succeeding generations. Looking at the past we see an unbroken chain of parents and young children, who in turn become parents – young children need older people to survive and grow up!

In Chapter 3 I develop the main theoretical framework of the book, arguing that sociologists investigating early childhood need to develop a relational approach that is multi-disciplinary, making important connections with other related disciplines, such as developmental psychology, social policy, history, anthropology, education and health. Sociologists of childhood need to integrate the biological and social aspects of young children's development, particularly overcoming some of their deepest fears and concerns about the role of developmental psychology.

Within this context, I discuss one of the most influential theories in developmental psychology – attachment. According to John Bowlby (2005), a young child needs a sensitive and responsive mother (or caretaker) for the development of emotional security. However, attachment theory can lead to an exclusive focus on adult–child interactions. I argue that it is still too narrowly based on the mother or parent dyad to capture the relational complexities of young children's social relationships with other significant people in their lives.

Institutionalisation of Childhood

The relative decline in male power and control over women and young children that has occurred in developed countries over the last 40 years has led to large numbers of women entering the part-time and full-time workforce. Both parents can be dual-earners, working full-time, earning a salary and pursuing their own careers. A useful comparison between the UK and Denmark highlights the differences in maternal employment between the two countries, especially for families with children under the age of five. Although the UK is quite generous in the time allocated for maternity leave (up to 52 weeks), much of it is unpaid, putting pressure on families' incomes. Denmark's parental leave benefits are more generous and flexible than the UK, and ensure that one parent can afford to remain at home with a young child over the first year of life, as well as enabling parents to share the childcare so that mothers can continue to invest in their careers. The provision of free or subsidised childcare is so important because it is an incentive to return to paid employment – in the UK, childcare costs are nearly three times more expensive than Denmark (OECD, 2012).

As more young children enter childcare and early education, the issue of transition from their immediate families to group care settings has grown in importance. Such developments make it even more vital to develop a sociological approach that can explain the changing institutional arrangements of care that young children experience. Institutional settings set the tone for the relationships between individual children, dyads (child–caregiver, peer–peer (friendships and playmates)) and group interactions between young children and their caregivers. Within this changing array of people young children learn about the membership rules of various networks.

An important consequence that stems from long hours of full-time paid employment by both parents is that many young children are spending more of their time during the day with childcare providers. In Chapter 4 I develop in more detail the theoretical argument of the book, using the work of the French sociologist Pierre Bourdieu to explore the significance of group processes (social habitus) in young children's relationships. The social habitus refers here to the internalisation of wider structures and processes manifested through the routines and taken-for-granted actions of young children: the longer a young child is located within a particular set of relationships the more likely they are to develop a practical sense of how to behave and act in certain ways.

We discuss the family as the 'primary habitus' or main institution where young children initially internalise ways of thinking and types of dispositions from their parents or carers. Although families are still important in the shaping of young children's lives, I argue that in contemporary society young children are not mere receptors of family socialisation, but active generators of their own social and cultural capital in early years settings. These settings can usefully be viewed within the concept of a shifting and competitive field, one that enables us to develop an understanding of when and where particular forms of capital become valued or diminish in importance and eventually decline.

Young Children's Play – Challenging the Adult Establishment

When young children spend time together over a long period, as they do in pre-school, they develop social capital in their own peer cultures. Being a pre-school child means that you are part of a very specific peer culture, holding unique, shared ideas of your own social position and status as well as that of your friends. Corsaro's (2005) concept of 'peer culture' is a vital step in overcoming a narrow instrumental view of play and can help us to explain young children's interpretations of their surrounding culture:

> The production of peer culture is a matter neither of simple interpretation nor of direct appropriation of the adult world. Children creatively appropriate information from the adult world to produce their own unique peer cultures. (Corsaro and Eder, 1990: 200)

In Chapter 5 I emphasise that young children's play should be framed within a relational context: young children create their own peer groups through the appropriation of adult-centred discourses but they do not mimic or passively accept the adult world. Their play stems from the tensions between their desire for relative independence from adults but their simultaneous dependence on them. I draw on the ideas of the German philosopher and literary critic Walter Benjamin (1892–1940) to develop an alternative version of play, one that explores the way in which young children's play is not simply an imitation of the real world but highly creative and transformative. Benjamin's perspective is important because it offers a relational approach for reconnecting the world of the adult and the young child by uncovering young children's alternative modes of seeing and knowing. His writings are an attempt to restore the earliest impressions of childhood which have not yet been tainted by the destructive adult power of habit.

One important way of beginning to understand how young children deeply engage with play is to focus on how they explore and challenge the rules and authority of adult culture. To understand how some of these aspects of play are enacted from a young child's perspective, I use the work of another twentieth-century literary critic, the Russian semiotician Mikhail Bakhtin (1895-1975). His concept of the carnival is used to explore the relational dynamics which shape children's relative independence from adults. In a similar way to the carnival, young children try to break down barriers and challenge power inequalities by mocking the hierarchical order established by parents and teachers – they attempt to resist authority and generate disorder to gain more control over their lives.

State Investment, Young Children and Families

In recent years OECD countries have increased their investment in early intervention and prevention initiatives targeted at young children and families (OECD, 2009). In the United Kingdom, New Labour targeted young children, families and disadvantaged communities to reduce social exclusion. The British government was concerned that vulnerable family formations were expanding at a faster rate than 'stable' family forms, and as a result increasing numbers of young children were not being adequately prepared for their future. This changing strategy in government can be understood as a broad approach that changed the focus from old notions of supporting families to making parents responsible for their own children (Rodger, 2012).

Compared to earlier prevention policies, recent British governments have promoted a more extensive preventative agenda, seeking social interventions to identify problems earlier and prevent them from getting worse and, even more ambitiously, to prevent problems from emerging: they have attempted to redefine the relationship between the state, young children and families with new forms of social support, intervention, regulation and surveillance (Little et al., 2002).

In Chapter 6 I argue that some of these changes in government policy towards contemporary families and the apparent 'parenting crisis' tend to be narrowly focused on short-term developments that need to be explained by long-term relational processes, based on changes in the balance of power between men, women and young children. Young children and parents increasingly live within families in highly interdependent relationships, where there are more and more pressures to control and regulate one's emotions and behaviour. According to Norbert Elias (2008), these changes can be explained by a longer trend of informalisation that has occurred from the late twentieth century onwards. This concept of informalisation refers to a period of movement from an authoritarian to a more egalitarian parent–child relationship where there is a loosening of barriers of authority in relations between young children and adults.

Investing in the Nation: Young Children's Health and Well-being

To briefly give an illustration of the way in which a relational approach to early childhood can be applied I will now discuss the historical development of state investment, looking at young children's health and well-being. Sociologists usually investigate their own present-day societies by mainly focusing on how the macro level of state investment in young children's services influences the finer detail of particular policies in their own nations (Pugh and Duffy, 2010). Even when comparative research is carried out, the dynamic relationships within and between different welfare states is rarely investigated (Lewis, 2008). However, the development of the modern welfare state was determined by its relations with other states. When two states or survival units struggle for survival – whether it is about prestige or scarce resources – they are dependent on each other (Kaspersen and Gabriel, 2008). The intensity of this struggle between different nation-states influences the internal welfare policies developed for young children and can be explained by the compelling force that groups within different societies exert upon each other (Elias, 2012).

In the latter half of the nineteenth and the early twentieth centuries, inter-state rivalry in different European countries was part of a wider dynamic relationship with crucial consequences for the health and well-being of young children. Rose (1990) draws attention to the importance of the young child as a primary national asset, arguing that the future strength of the nation-state became dependent upon the vitality and development of young children:

> In different ways, at different times, and by many different routes varying from one section of society to another, the health, welfare, and rearing of children has been linked in thought and practice to the destiny of the nation and the responsibilities of the state. (1990: 121)

During a period of growing nationalism and imperialist wars, the health and fitness of the population became an important concern for different national governments. In England, the health of adult men was brought to light by the Boer War (1899–1902) when two out of five of those who volunteered to go to fight in South Africa were rejected because of poor physique (Cunningham, 2006). The poor level of recruitment and under-performance of the British army were seen as an urgent national problem which was linked to the poor health of young children (Hendrick, 1994). The physical condition of the population was first raised by the Interdepartmental Committee on Physical Deterioration in 1904 and again in five further government reports between 1910 and 1916.

And this was not solely a British concern because during this time Britain's main imperialist rival was Germany. Heywood (2001) notes that in 1906 the medical expert Arthur Schlossman explained in a speech that tackling high infant mortality rates needed to be given a high priority since an increase in population would contribute to Germany's military strength, its labour force and its consumption. The infant mortality rate is defined by the number of children who die aged less than one year old per 1,000 births. A lower infant mortality rate can indicate that better care is being taken of children and is linked to several factors, including access to health care services for pregnant mothers and infants, the socio-economic status of the child's parents, the health of the mother, low birth weight and preterm birth.

Hendrick (1997) has thus identified the end of the nineteenth century up until the end of the First World War (1880-1914) as a cru-cial period in child welfare reform and policy because there was a shift of emphasis from child protection to national issues of efficiency and health, focusing on the physical and mental development of young chil-dren. This was linked to the scientific study of young children through the development of particular disciplines, particularly those based upon developmental thinking about the 'normal' child. Rose (1990), drawing on the work of the French philosopher Michel Foucault, argues that the concept of the 'normal child' functioned in three ways: between factual claims and normative assertions, so that what is perceived to be natural is considered healthy; a standard against which young children are judged; and an objective to be achieved through social policies and programmes.

Foucault, Discourse and Power

It is not an uncommon assumption for us to think of power as something politicians exercise at a local, governmental or national level. At the top of the hierarchy are influential politicians with 'absolute' power and the rest of the population with hardly any. This is usually referred to as a zero-sum situation. But this common-sense approach focuses too narrowly on 'political' power – there are other important relational aspects of power that stem from economic, military, ideological and professional sources. This interpretation is also quite misleading because power is involved in all human relationships – it is influenced by complex sets of relationships which are finely balanced and subject to continuous change.

According to Foucault, we are all actively involved in and governed by power relationships. He viewed power as local and dispersed: similar to a colour dye, it operates through the entire social structure and is embedded in the daily practices of professions. Power produces practices in many fields, determining how problems are constituted, how people are classified and what are considered appropriate ways to shape behaviour. For him it becomes an imperative to unmask the working of power relations, 'to show that things are not as self-evident as one believed, to see that what is accepted as self-evident will no longer be accepted as such' (Foucault, 1988: 155).

Discourse is one of the key concepts that Foucault introduces to explain how power becomes legitimised. The language we use shapes and directs our way of looking at and understanding the world, exercising power over our thought by governing what we see as the truth and how we understand the world. Foucault calls such conventions - our way of naming things and talking about them – *discourses*, and those discourses that exercise a decisive influence on a specific practice can be seen as 'dominant discursive regimes' or 'regimes of truth'. Such regimes serve a disciplinary or regulatory function: they can be used to explain the relationship between discourses on early childhood and the exercise of professional power of a wide range of experts (for example, health visitors, social workers, doctors and nurses) who become involved in the scrutiny of and intervention in the lives of young children.

In Chapter 7 I discuss how childhood and sexuality share a similar historical discourse with that of the eighteenth century – they are crucial dimensions in the contemporary Western definition of childhood and adulthood, maintaining boundaries between them and fuelling debates about the moral dangers of new technologies such as the Internet. I argue that by separating young children from the adult sphere of life and denying them participation in the discourses through which we understand sexuality, adults make young children even more vulnerable to the desires of others. Sexuality is not just knowledge that adults find problematic and uncomfortable, but is built upon relations of power between adults and young children that are maintained and reproduced within society.

Conclusion

This introduction has discussed some of the key themes and chapters that will be developed throughout the book. I have emphasised that a sociological approach to early childhood must be relational in two important ways. First, young children are born into interdependent relationships that existed before them: as they grow up these relationships change but are structured in different societies and in different historical epochs. Second, in order to develop a strong sociology of early childhood, a range of relational perspectives will be used from other disciplines in the social sciences. The next chapter will focus on the important contribution of one key social science discipline, history. I will discuss how historians of childhood began to challenge conventional views on children, paving the way for the development of new sociological perspectives on childhood.

DISCUSSION ACTIVITY

Read carefully the following quotation from the French novelist Georges Perec:

My childhood belongs to those things which I know I don't know much about. It is behind me; yet it is the ground on which I grew, and it once belonged to me, however obstinately I assert that it no longer does. ... However, childhood is neither longing nor terror, neither a paradise lost or the Golden Fleece, but maybe it is a horizon, a point of departure, a set of co-ordinates from which the axes of my life may draw their meaning. (Perec, 2011: 12)

Consider the following questions:

1. How does Perec remember his early childhood?

2. In what ways have your own memories of your earliest years influenced you?

3. 'Childhood is a point of departure' – how can we explain the relationship between early childhood and adulthood?

Further Reading

Interview with Michel Foucault: http://www.michaelbess.org/foucault-interview/

This accessible interview with Foucault ('Power, Moral Values, and the Intellectual', *History of the Present* 4 (Spring 1988), 1-2, 11-13) was conducted on 3 November 1980, by Michael Bess, a graduate student in the Department of History at the University of California, Berkeley. One important aspect of this interview to note is the way that Foucault views power as a set of very complex relations which guide 'the behaviour of others' and 'demand infinite reflections'.

A. de Swaan (2001) Chapter 5, 'How People Form One Another: Socialisation and Civilisation', in *Human Societies: An Introduction*. Cambridge: Polity.

This beautifully written book is a brief introduction to the study of society that may be read without any previous knowledge of the social sciences. De Swaan's engaging style of writing is lucid and jargon-free – each chapter addresses a fundamental question about people in their various arrangements. Chapter 5 examines the learning processes of young children, what they need to learn to survive in different societies and how they become civilised in contemporary society.

S. Efrat Efron (2008) 'Moral Education between Hope and Hopelessness: The Legacy of Janusz Korczak', *Curriculum Inquiry*, 38(1): 39–62.

This article is about Janusz Korczak (1878–1942), a radical Jewish-Polish educator who for more than 30 years devoted his life to educating orphaned Jewish and non-Jewish children. During the Second World War, he stayed with the Jewish children to the end as they all perished in a concentration camp. The orphanages he directed were democratic, self-ruled communities, where the children had their own parliament, court and newspaper. In these institutions relational bonds were highly emphasised in every aspect of community life: 'When I play or talk with a child, two equally mature moments, mine and the child's, intertwine' (Korczak, 1992: 179).

References

Bowlby, J. (2005) *A Secure Base*. London: Routledge.

Corsaro W. (2005) *The Sociology of Childhood*, 2nd edition. Thousand Oaks, CA: Pine Forge Press.

Corsaro, W.A. and Eder, D. (1990) 'Children's Peer Cultures', *Annual Review of Sociology*, 16: 197–220.

Cunningham, H. (2006) *The Invention of Childhood*. London: BBC.

Dahlberg, G. and Moss, P. (2005) *Ethics and Politics in Early Childhood Education*. London: RoutledgeFalmer.

Dahlberg, G., Moss, P. and Pence, A. (1999) *Beyond Quality in Early Childhood Education and Care: Postmodern Perspectives*. London: Falmer Press.

Dépelteau, F. and Powell, C. (2013) (eds) *Applying Relational Sociology: Relations, Networks and Society*. New York: Palgrave Macmillan.

De Swaan, A. (1990) *The Management of Normality: Critical Essays in Health and Welfare*. London: Routledge.

Elias, N. (2008) 'The Civilising of Parents', in *Essays II: On Civilising Processes, State Formation and National Identity*. Dublin: UCD Press [The Collected Works of Norbert Elias, vol. 15], pp. 14–40.

Elias, N. (2012) *What is Sociology?* Dublin: UCD Press [Collected Works, vol. 5].

Farrell, A., Kagan, S.L. and Tisdall, E.K.M. (2015) *The SAGE Handbook of Early Childhood Research*. London: Sage.

Feynman, R.P. (1988) *'What Do You Care What Other People Think?' Further Adventures of a Curious Character*. New York: W.W. Norton.

Foucault, M. (1988) 'Critical Theory/Intellectual Theory', interview with Gerard Raulet, in L. Kritzman (ed.), *Michel Foucault: Politics, Philosophy, Culture: Interviews and Other Writings, 1977–1984*. London: Routledge.

Hendrick, H. (1994) *Child Welfare: England, 1872–1989*. London: Routledge.

Hendrick, H. (1997) *Children, Childhood and English Society, 1880–1990*. Cambridge: Cambridge University Press.

Heywood, C. (2001) *A History of Childhood: Children and Childhood in the West from Medieval to Modern Times*. Cambridge: Polity Press.

Kaspersen, L.B. and Gabriel, N. (2008) 'The Importance of Survival Units for Norbert Elias's Figurational Perspective', *Sociological Review*, 56(3): 370–387.

Korczak, J. (1992) *When I Am Little Again* (E.P. Kulawiec, trans.). In *When I Am Little Again and Child's Right to Respect*. Lanham, MD: University Press of America, pp. 3–158.

Lewis, J. (ed.) (2008) *Children, Changing Families and Welfare States*. Cheltenham: Edward Elgar.

Little, M., Axford, N. and Morpeth, L. (2002) 'Research Review: Risk and Protection in the (1) Context of Services for Children in Need', *Child and Family Social Work*, 9: 105–117.

OECD (2009) *Doing Better for Children*. Paris: OECD.

OECD (2012) OECD Family Database, www.oecd.org/social/family/database

Osgood, J. (2010) 'Reconstructing Professionalism in ECEC: The Case for the "Critically Reflective Emotional Professional"', *Early Years: An International Research Journal*, 30(2): 119–133.

Perec, G. (2011) *W or The Memory of Childhood*. London: Vintage.

Pugh, G. and Duffy, B. (eds) (2010) *Contemporary Issues in the Early Years*, 5th edition. London: Sage.

Rodger, J.J. (2012) '"Regulating the Poor": Observations on the "Structural Coupling" of Welfare, Criminal Justice and the Voluntary Sector in a "Big Society"', *Social Policy and Administration*, 46(4): 413–443.

Rose, N. (1990) *Governing the Soul*. London: Routledge.

2

HISTORICAL AND SOCIOLOGICAL PERSPECTIVES ON CHILDHOOD

Introduction

In an evocative introduction to *A Little History of the World*, the art historian Ernst Gombrich (2008: 1) strongly conveys to his young readers the long chain of generational relationships. He emphasises the way in which we are all interconnected – we can go further and further back throughout history, tracing a long line of descendants. Behind every 'once upon a time', there is always another: 'Once upon a time there was a small boy – or a small girl …'. Your father and mother were also small once, and so was your grandfather, and your grandmother… But they too had grandfathers and grandmothers, and they too could say: 'Once upon a time'. We often look to our own childhoods as a measure by which comparisons between past and present might be made. Yet very often memories of this period in our lives become imbued with nostalgia, or, where too painful to recall, they are shaped by our understanding of acceptable early childhood experiences. The great Dutch cultural historian Johan Huizinga (1872–1945) used the concept of 'historical sensation' to draw attention to the importance of direct contact through the feeling of personal involvement in a past event, a person's history or a historical remnant.

When, for example, I turn to my own childhood growing up in Glasgow, I initially think of a wonderful time for play and adventure with close friends. But then I stop. I was about four and playing on my bicycle with my best friend Kenneth when he said he could no longer play with me because I was different. I did not understand what he was saying, so I asked what he meant. He told me I was Jewish. I ran home crying, telling my Mum and Dad what had happened. They reassured me that being Jewish was not terrible – I was beginning to learn what it felt like to be different.

So how do we understand our own and other people's history? Initially, this may seem a relatively simple question. It is tempting to answer that history is concerned with people and events in the past. But what criteria should we use to select past events and different groups of people who may have been important in shaping these events? A good starting point is the definition of history given by the very influential social historian E.H. Carr (1987: 29–30) in his path-breaking book *What is History?* Carr stated that history is 'An unending dialogue between the present and the past', arguing that history was concerned with neither the intentions of individual great men or women, nor the listing of unique events, but the interpretation and explanation of social patterns and regularities. By looking at long-term developments, especially how economic and social forces influence contemporary social problems, we may be in a better position to understand how these social patterns connect our past with our present.

Despite this turn to social history, prior to the 1970s very little had been written about children as people or childhood as a concept. According to Morrison (2012), four factors influenced the new historical research on children. First, demographers became interested in children when they became aware that population studies should include birth rates, death rates, infanticide and abortion. Second, there was a new curiosity amongst historians to move from the study of social classes to smaller social groups who fell outside pre-defined socio-economic categories. Third, the influence of Foucault drew attention to the 'normalising' discourses in institutions that young children internalise as part of their behaviour (see the previous discussion in Chapter 1). Lastly, feminists began to investigate the formation of female and male identity, raising questions about how these identities are shaped in early childhood.

This chapter will introduce you to some of the major historical approaches to childhood that have provided a great deal of detailed knowledge about children in different periods of human history. Since the publication of Philippe Ariès' (1962) groundbreaking *Centuries of Childhood*, historians of childhood have identified major research areas such as the representation of the child, advice literature for the care of children, the transition from child labour to schooling and the development of social welfare policies. They have emphasised the importance of placing children centre stage in their analysis, exploring how childhood as a key concept has shaped the way that children are perceived as different from adults.

This historical context provides a key foundation to understand the major contributions that, during the last 40 years, have contributed to the debate about the importance of including children within a sociological perspective. I will discuss the key assumptions that lie behind the major sociological theories on childhood that emerged in the 1970s and early 1980s, exploring how they became influential in the social studies of childhood. In this perspective, childhood is not a universal concept, but a social construction of the specific ways in which young children become socialised in different societies. Sociologists of childhood have emphasised how children construct their own lives, exploring some of the unequal power relationships that they face as they grow up in different societies. In my conclusion, I argue that we need to build upon some of the important insights from the sociology and historiography of childhood to develop a relational sociology of early childhood, one that offers a strong foundation for interdisciplinary and cross-disciplinary collaboration.

Ariès and the Historiography of Childhood

Leading British historians of childhood such as Heywood (2010) and Cunningham (2005) have acknowledged that the starting point for the history of childhood was the publication of Ariès' (1962) *Centuries of Childhood*. It was the first work to historicise childhood, to suggest that childhood was not a 'natural' or 'universal' phenomenon, but one that varied according to time and place. In taking their inspiration from Ariès, historians gathered together a range of material on past constructions of childhood, interpreting it as a short or long period, or as a stage of life that was either despised or venerated by adults.

Heywood (2010) identifies three key arguments from *Centuries of Childhood* that we will discuss and then assess in the light of recent historical research. The first is the oft-quoted line that 'in medieval society the idea of childhood did not exist' (Ariès, 1962: 125). Before the fifteenth century, there was little collective awareness of children as different – from the age of seven they were considered as smaller adults. Ariès based his argument on an extensive analysis of paintings and iconography, where there were very few representations of the uniqueness of children, 'They have simply been depicted on a smaller scale' (Ariès, 1962: 31). He drew from other sources, notably clothing, games and attitudes to sexuality to argue that children after the age of three or four played the same games as everyone else, either among themselves or with adults. Children were to be found gambling at cards and playing tennis and hockey, while adults cheerfully joined in snowball fights or games of blind-man's buff. Courtiers even played sexual games with the future French king Louis XIII, fondling his privates and making jokes about his future wife when he was still an infant.

The second key argument is that in the late sixteenth and seventeenth centuries there began the 'discovery of childhood', spread over a long period of at least four centuries. It started with the 'coddling' of children during the fourteenth and fifteenth centuries, taking a delight in their company, moving on to its discovery by a small group of reformers, composed of priests, lawyers and 'moralists', who understood the innocence and weakness of young children. Notions of children's special nature and needs called for special attention to their emotional development in the home and for formal education in the school aimed at preparing children for the transition to an adult world. Ariès argued that the very short childhood of the past, ending around the age of seven, gave way to the modern concept of a long childhood.

The third and last key part of Ariès' argument is that with the modern conception of childhood there emerged a new conception of the family: the return of children to their families was a 'great event' of the seventeenth century, one that transformed parent–child relations. He discussed a long and complicated shift from the medieval family concerned with problems such as the honour of the line, to the modern family, focused exclusively on the relationship between parents and children. In the medieval period children left their families at an early age, weakening their emotional bonds with their parents, but with the rise of the bourgeois family, middle-class parents became more concerned with developing intimate relationships at home.

Ariès' thesis was critically scrutinised by other historians in relation to its historical method, interpretation and the evidence that lay behind his claims, particularly his contention that a fundamental historical change in parent–child relations occurred (see the influential study by Pollock [1983]). Early in his book he uses the terms 'indifference' and 'callousness' in his discussion of attitudes towards children, which he linked directly to the high infant and child mortality of the medieval and early modern periods. He believed that parents could not allow themselves to become too attached to children they were very likely to lose. In marked contrast, by the seventeenth century the family had become secure in the privacy of its home and the care given to children made it possible for a new emotional attitude to emerge. It is important to note, however, that Ariès stated that the absence of a concept of childhood in medieval society was still compatible with affection for children – it did not mean that children were 'neglected, forsaken or despised' (1962: 128).

Ariès drew on the inability of artists to paint children, depicting them as miniature adults, as evidence for the absence of the modern concept of childhood. But does the absence of children in paintings necessarily reflect a lack of care or concern for their welfare? Fuller (1979) has pointed out that paintings of children as miniature adults were mainly depictions of the dominant classes in society – parents were keen to display the future power and wealth of their children. Orme (2001) has also argued that from the thirteenth to the fifteenth centuries, there was a growing interest in drawing and painting the young reflected in everyday life, as children fell into wells or fires, suffered beatings from parents and schoolteachers, played with their friends, studied in class – or were led away by the Grim Reaper.

Nevertheless, historians such as Shorter (1977) and Stone (1979) supported the idea of a dramatic change in parent–child relations during the early modern period and were clear that the modern approach was an improvement on the traditional one. Influenced by Ariès, both emphasised a warmer, more affectionate family environment as economic interest was replaced by the importance of emotion. E.P. Thompson (1977: 501), the well-known Marxist historian, offered a devastating critique of their approach:

> It annoys me that both Professor Stone and Professor Shorter leave their readers to feel so complacent about their own modernity. It annoys me even more that both should indict the poor, on so little evidence, of indifference to their children and of callous complicity in their high rate of mortality ... But if the lower orders had not formed some kind of affective bonding and familial loyalty, we, their descendants, might never have made our gracious descent.

Cunningham (2005) adds another important contribution to this debate by situating childhood and the family within a broader social context. He points to the trend in the West in the late nineteenth and early twentieth centuries in which the length of childhood began to be extended through the introduction and enforcement of mass compulsory schooling. With the development of the welfare state and philanthropic intervention, a common experience of childhood for all children emerged.

This development led to one of the most important shifts in the experience of childhood, from one where nearly all children expected to contribute to the family economy at an early age to one where they were a 'net drain' on that economy throughout their childhood.

This shift in the length and nature of childhood has been brought out vividly in Zelizer's (1994) influential study in the historiography of childhood. She explored how the valuation of children changed from one where they were valued according to their contributions to the family economy to one where they became productively useless but emotionally priceless – the more emotionally valuable they became for adults, the longer in life they were likely to be perceived as children.

Past and Present Images of Childhood

In this section, I draw attention to some of the difficulties in conducting historical research, discussing how issues can be selected and evaluated solely from the standpoint of what is regarded as important by historians in contemporary societies. These contemporary circumstances can determine how and what we see as history. Let us now investigate in a little more detail the complex relationships between past and present and some of the problems in historical interpretation. From his stance in mid-twentieth-century bourgeois France, Ariès sought to understand how a particular set of beliefs about childhood and practices of childrearing had come about. But when he looked for evidence of our twentieth-century conception of childhood in medieval Europe and failed to find it, he jumped to the conclusion that it did not exist. In historical analysis, it is sometimes all too easy to be influenced by the partiality of one's own feelings and the values of today's society.

Müller (2009) argues that contemporary historians of childhood have been far too influenced by the ideals of their time, discovering a Romantic version of childhood that emphasises innocence: children need special attention, care and protection through family, schools and legal regulations and thus their childhood is cherished as a 'natural' form of existence with which most adults have lost touch. She contends that a modern version of an innocent childhood has perpetuated a Romantic myth about the discovery of childhood in the latter decades of the eighteenth century – the child of the Romantics was considered to be pure and innocent, a creature of nature and simplicity, yet at the same time innately pious, standing as a beacon of hope in an increasingly disordered world.

Because there is always the problem that historical fragments are left to the discretion of the individual researcher, we need to be constantly aware of some of the underlying assumptions that historians bring to interpret their selected texts. Frijhoff (2012) therefore suggests that the historical entanglement of childhood and the self needs to be kept at a distance because the discovery of childhood can easily evolve into a personal discovery of ourselves – the values of the historical child can easily be transferred to the modern historian and vice versa. He believes that the real problem for the historian of childhood is to remain faithful to the categories of the past as well as to the present, but without fully identifying with the child that has been. This is a difficult balancing act, because our emotions and memories are involved – our own memories of having been a young child remain a central part of who we think we are and who we think we once were. Remembering our childhood commonly calls to mind Romantic fantasies of play and adventure: the conviction that young children belong out of doors and in nature marks these contemporary discourses as continuous with a long tradition of representations of desirable childhoods in Western European societies.

Some of the important contradictions in Romantic notions of childhood can be observed in what Cunningham (1991) has described as the heroic story of child rescue. (The continuing influence of the Romantic discourse on childhood will be further explored in Chapter 6.) 'Child-saving' as discourse and practice drew impetus from numerous social surveys of urban poverty published by Victorian commentators, which included graphic accounts of young children's lives on the street. Recurrent motifs focused on the sensory assault of the streets and gutters, for example from the 'odorous dirt' (Archer, 1870). Depictions of street life collided with Romantic views of the child emanating from Rousseau and writers such as William Blake and William Wordsworth. In his Ode, *Intimations of Immortality from Recollections of Early Childhood*, Wordsworth proclaimed 'Heaven lies about us in our infancy!' (1888).

These Romantic ideas located the child not in the gutter of a city street but in the natural environment of field and forest. In the context of the city, relocation of the child was to be within a garden. Margaret McMillan's visionary conception of the garden found practical expression from 1917 in the Rachel McMillan Open-Air Nursery School in Deptford, a 'suitable provocative environment' (McMillan, 1930: 78), providing opportunities for developing young children's physical, mental and moral well-being and risk-taking. Writers and artists responded to the sharp division between these Romantic representations and the actualities of life on the streets by engaging in 'child-saving', setting up new organisations concerned with preventing cruelty to young children. Examples are the work of Barnardo, who opened his first boys' home in 1870, and the National Society for the Protection of Cruelty to Children (NSPCC), which became a national body in 1889.

Swain (2009) argues that while emotive images of a 'childhood lost' were highly effective in encouraging supporters to rescue young children, there is little evidence that child rescuers believed that the children amongst whom they worked could, or should, aspire to the idealised childhood which was depicted in much of the fictional, juvenile and guidance literature of the time. Although they used the notion of a lost childhood to argue that it was in the best interests of the child to be removed from parents or guardians, the future they offered the young children they rescued was one that served to perpetuate the inequalities which lay at the centre of their distress.

Disempowered, cut off from their families and communities, and trained for a life of servitude, their childhoods were shaped primarily by labour, with love dependent on chance or good fortune. More importantly, survivor narratives, whether in family histories, published autobiographies or evidence before government enquiries, all testified to the vulnerability of the 'rescued' child and the prevalence of physical and sexual abuse in the cottages and foster or adoptive homes in which they were placed (see, for example, Australian Senate Community Affairs References Committee, 2001).

Social Constructions of Childhood

The sociologists Alan Prout and Allison James noted that history was one of the first disciplines to take up new directions in the study of childhood during the 1970s. They emphasised the work of Ariès for the way his interpretation of childhood during the medieval period provided an important example of its variability in human societies. 'Ariès's challenge to orthodoxy', they wrote, 'lay in his suggestion that the concept of childhood emerged in Europe between the fifteenth and eighteenth centuries, thus blasting a large hole in traditional assumptions about the universality of childhood' (Prout and James, 1997: 16). They were aware of the contentious nature of Ariès' work, but insisted that 'the particular form of modern childhood is historically specific' (Prout and James, 1997: 17).

The emergence of the social construction of childhood should be viewed as a response to the dominant intellectual trends in developmental child psychology and structural-functionalist theories of socialisation (James and Prout, 1997; James et al., 1998). Within developmental psychology, what was important was finding ways of turning the immature, irrational and incompetent child into a mature, rational and competent adult. These dominant principles at the heart of developmental psychology have been referred to by Smart et al. (2001) as the embryonic model – one where young children are considered to be in a state of permanent transition, either within or between stages.

One of the key thinkers in developmental psychology was Piaget (1970). In Piaget's framework children's intellectual development is compared to an evolutionary process, one in which the later stages of development succeed earlier ones because they are more adequate to reality. Development is viewed as a self-regulating interaction between the child and the physical and social environment, which gives rise to new forms of knowledge. As they progress through a series of sequentially linked stages, children gradually learn the cognitive skills involved with reasoning, logic, causality and morality until they achieve adulthood.

In the structural-functionalist writings of the 1950s and 1960s, particularly in the work of Parsons (1951), socialisation became defined as a psychological process whereby the young child learns the 'laid-down' patterns of values that will mould them to fit into existing society. For sociologists, the aim of socialisation theory was to explain the transmission of culture from one generation to another by the key institutions of community, education and the family (see Elkin and Handel, 1972). Learning to conform to social rules, young children gradually acquire knowledge of the roles needed for adult life.

A New Paradigm for the Sociology of Childhood

As originally formulated by James and Prout (1997: 8–9) I will now discuss the six key assumptions of their new paradigm:

(1) Childhood is understood as a social construction

A key aspect in James and Prout's (1997) framework is their commitment to developing a more sensitive awareness of different versions of childhood and children's experiences as they construct their own lives. They have criticised the belief that there exists one universal childhood, a 'standard' childhood that is based on the experiences of children in developed countries. They have pointed out that it is biological immaturity rather than childhood that is a universal feature of human groups. To overcome the problems of assuming that children are the same throughout the world, it is important to take into consideration the different cultural contexts of children growing up in different countries. Wyness (2006: 23) provides a good summary of the argument that 'biology' and 'culture' should be separated in the social construction of childhood:

[W]hat sociologists of childhood argue is that children's biological differences from adults need to be separated from the cultural components of childhood. The idea that children are commonly believed to be morally and culturally weaker or less significant than adults does not necessarily indicate that this incapacity or subordination is based on their physiological or biological weakness. Children in different historical and cultural contexts are quite capable of actions that belie their physiological immaturity.

(2) Childhood is a variable of social analysis

Childhood is intimately connected with other variables such as class, gender and ethnicity, and therefore a comparative, cultural analysis can enable us to identify a variety of different childhoods. James and James (2004) developed the notion of the cultural politics of childhood – the influence of political processes through which childhood is constructed in different societies at different times (see also the very influential edited collection of papers by Sharon Stephens, *Children and the Politics of Culture* [1995]).

The extent to which young children can participate in political processes can also help us to reconsider the ways in which they are excluded (Mayall, 2012). This is particularly important as assumptions about the 'global' child stem from the perspective of the Minority World countries (children from developed countries, mainly living in Europe and North America), where parents and governments are encouraged to protect children. These Minority World assumptions are not universal, but are defined by very particular features of an appropriate childhood such as not participating in any kind of paid work. In the Majority World large numbers of young children do work, do not live with their biological parents or are excluded through social class, ethnicity or gender. Although charities like Save the Children have for a long time been involved in raising funds to rescue street children and child labourers in the Majority World (children from the developing countries of Asia, Africa and Latin America where the majority of young children live) young children's experiences on the street and in work are much more complex than the campaigns suggest (Wells, 2009).

(3) Children's social relationships and cultures are worthy of study in their own right

There are two key traditions in the study of childhood cultures. The first tradition is the exploration of peer-to-peer transmitted culture. Children's folklore studies have explored street culture, playground games and rhymes and orally transmitted stories such as urban legends and ghost stories (Tucker, 2008). The second more recent body of work has examined children's popular culture in the light of their engagement with a variety of media and new technologies (Drotner and Livingstone, 2008). Despite the longstanding acknowledgement by children's folklore scholars of the relationship between popular culture and children's historical cultural traditions (Opie and Opie, 1959), these two areas of childhood culture have frequently been separated and presented as morally, ethically and commercially different (Kline, 1993).

The romanticisation of traditional childhood pursuits such as outdoor play and play with non-commercial toys has led to recurrent condemnation of aspects of children's media culture (Palmer, 2006), despite calls to move beyond these simplistic binaries (Buckingham, 2000).

According to Marsh (2010: 17), 'childhood culture is contemporaneously constructed by children and shaped by adult interests and it is the tensions between these processes that lead to creativity and innovation'. In Chapter 5 I argue that we need to explore how young children develop their own play within a relational frame of analysis, which is followed by my later discussion in Chapter 7 of how new media technologies such as the Internet have become an important part of young children's lives in today's society.

(4) Children are and must be seen as active in the construction and determination of their own social lives, the lives of those around them and of the societies in which they live

A key weakness in the structural-functionalist perspective was the major assumption that the child is 'mere putty to be worked on by external forces' (Richards, 1974: 4). Researchers working in the new social studies of childhood that emerged in the 1970s and early 1980s began to rethink childhood and challenge this view that young children were mere passive recipients of socialisation (Richards, 1974). Sociologists of childhood (see in particular, James and Prout, 1997; Mayall, 2002) emphasised the present tense of childhood, children's active participation in constructing their own lives and their relationships with parents and friends. They argued that in the early years of human life a different framework is needed to understand the institution of childhood: 'children are not formed by natural and social forces but rather ... they inhabit a world of meaning created by themselves and through their interaction with adults' (James et al., 1998: 28).

(5) Ethnography is a particularly useful methodology for the study of childhood

According to McNamee and Seymour (2012: 164), the defining feature of the new social study of childhood is its use of a participatory methodology, based on the development of child-friendly methods for working directly with young children. There has been a paradigm shift in the social study of childhood from traditional research methods using measurement, observation and testing to those that focus on the child as subject, relational and situated within a generational order. (The important concept of generation in developing a relational sociology as will be discussed in the section on Universality of Childhood.) This epistemological shift required the inclusion of some techniques previously considered inappropriate for use with children such as questionnaires, interviews and discussions, vignettes, participant observation, written accounts and diaries. New techniques such as structured activities, audio, photographic and visual recording and walkabouts were developed which not only challenged the 'unequal relationships between children and adults', but the more dominant sociological approaches to methods (Lange and Mierendorff, 2009: 91). Important methodological debates have also arisen about the extent to which researching with young children is similar to or different from researching with adults (Tisdall et al., 2009); ethical issues (Alderson and Morrow, 2011); the development of innovative methods and tools (Thomson, 2008); and the extent to which young children are active participants in the research process (Ennew and Watson, 2009).

(6) The process of reconstructing childhood

The development of a new sociology of childhood has become closely related with the United Nations Convention on the Rights of the Child (UNCRC). Passed by the UN Assembly in 1989, the UNCRC's 54 articles cover civil, economic, social and cultural rights for children and young people. We can view the Convention as providing a framework for three overarching and interconnected principles: the best interests of the child (Article 3); the non-discrimination principle (Article 2); and respect for the views of the child (Article 12). They can also be divided into the three Ps: protection – children should be protected from neglect, abuse, exploitation and discrimination; provision – children should have rights to necessary goods, services and resources; and participation - children should be respected as active members of their family, community and society, contributing from their earliest years. International donors like UNICEF have developed policies based on children's rights and there is growing pressure on governments and non-governmental organisations to promote and implement them throughout the world.

However, there are a number of major issues or disputes surrounding how we, as adults, view children's rights and how children can empower themselves. Children's liberation is one of the key disputes and child liberationists like Holt (1975) have advocated children's rights to self-determination, which includes enabling them to act and choose for themselves, to vote, work, own property, choose their own guardian and make sexual choices. He contends that age is an arbitrary criterion, unjustly depriving children of their rights because they are falsely believed to be incompetent and unable to make informed decisions. On the other hand, those who propose the caretaker thesis oppose the right to children's self-determination, arguing that children should not be free to make autonomous decisions: adults should make decisions on behalf of children and in their best interests (see Purdy, 1992). Underlying this thesis is the assumption that all adults are capable of making rational, autonomous decisions and young children are incapable because they are wild, variable and emotionally inconsistent. Protection by adults operates here as a form of social control by preventing young children from making their own decisions.

Theoretical Limitations in the Sociology of Childhood

Prout (2005) has argued that though researchers working within the new social studies of childhood have been productive, there are intellectual limitations in their research programme, which is based upon a set of oppositional dichotomies. Their theoretical framework assumes that childhood is a social construction which stands in opposition to older biologically centred ideas of childhood. This was understandable in the formative stage of the approach's development, because in order to establish their distinct contribution, novel intellectual initiatives frequently overstate their case, emphasising their differences from previous formulations.

Prout (2005, 2011) contends that the narrowness of such dichotomies, including the placing of psychology against sociology, are symptomatic of the modernist agenda in childhood studies. There is a tendency towards separating the social and cultural aspects of childhood from the biological ones. Influenced by the European philosophers Deleuze and Guattari (1988), Prout argues that the previous established sociology of childhood was situated in a binary logic that examines childhood through the lens of either culture or nature. The problems that this creates are usually dealt with in one of two ways. The first is reductionist: the attempt to explain all aspects of childhood in terms of a single principle, either biological or social. The second is additive: nature and culture remain as separate, incommensurable entities that are then seen as contributing a distinct proportion of the material that goes into the construction of childhood. The discussion is then about the proportion of each that goes into the mixture. Both the reductionist and the additive approach encourage the study of childhood to proceed on separate social and biological tracks.

To further develop the field, Prout (2005) believes that it is necessary to reconnect the social study of childhood with those aspects of earlier or different approaches that have something valuable to offer. However illuminating it is to regard childhood as a social phenomenon, it is not and never has been purely 'social'. Social relations are already heterogeneous, that is, they are made up from a wide variety of material, discursive, cultural, natural, technological, human and non-human resources. According to Prout, childhood is heterogeneous, complex and emergent and therefore its understanding requires a broad set of intellectual resources, an interdisciplinary approach combined with an open-minded process of enquiry.

Lee and Motzkau (2011) have also attempted to overcome this problem of separating the biological from the social or 'bio-social dualism' by developing a framework of three 'multiplicities' (Deleuze and Guattari, 1988), which they refer to as 'life', 'resource' and 'voice'. Each multiplicity is the historical product of the mutual development of research and governmental activity surrounding childhood during the twentieth century and can be seen as a summary of the major sensitivities that mainstream childhood research developed during this period. Together they map the main contours of states and researchers' relations with childhood. National concerns about young children's well-being have long been intimately connected with large-scale investment by European states. Such concerns led to the development of the Infant Welfare Movement in the UK, with its emphasis on the physical aspects of child development and public health. At the heart of this movement was a network of voluntary facilities, clinics and welfare provisions whose main objective was to promote 'mothercraft', helping mothers to nurse their infants in their own homes (Hendrick, 2003).

Each multiplicity is composed of articulations among a range of events and processes that cross conventional disciplinary boundaries. 'Life' is about biological processes but it is not just about the development of individual children. It also touches on such disciplines as demographics and epidemiology. Crucially, this multiplicity is composed of more or less successful articulations of events and processes that are biological, medical, legal, ethical and political. Similarly, 'resource' involves the politically informed range of decisions that are made regarding the value and use of children by states. Questions of children's agency often focus on what resources are available to them and the extent to which they are free to relate to themselves and to others as a 'resource'. The multiplicity of 'voice' concerns the ethical and political aspects of young children's representation and participation (Hart, 2007) and the many circumstances in which they can and cannot find voice, along with the range of institutional and technological conditions in which their voices are interpreted, mediated and amplified (Motzkau, 2010). Attempts to articulate events and processes involving young children in order to compose politically effective representations have been key processes in the formation of this multiplicity.

Similarly Taylor (2011) tries to bring a fresh new perspective on the relationship between two commonly conflated concepts 'childhood' and 'nature' by drawing upon developments in human geography. She suggests that although childhood studies scholars have gone a long way towards re-theorising childhood beyond the 'natural' and the 'universal' by pointing to its historical and cultural construction, they have not paid enough attention to the key concept of nature. (In Chapter 6 I return to this key concept by discussing how it has been used to inform and shape changing historical beliefs about the best way for parents to bring up young children.)

In response to Latour's (2005) calls to recast nature within a new multi-natural collective politics and Donna Haraway's (2008) project to queer what counts as nature, geographers have promoted a relational understanding of nature and culture. Within human geography, examples of this new relational theorising include queering nature/culture boundaries within 'situated' natures (Instone, 2004) and reconceptualising geography as 'entanglements of nature and culture' (Harrison et al., 2004). What they share is an understanding of the interdependencies of the human and the more-than-human worlds. From this basis human geographers approach nature as a collective – a network, an assemblage or an imbroglio – of all living and inert things, including human and non-human animals, objects and discursive practices.

Taylor (2011) argues that this relational perspective opens up new grounds for reconceptualising childhood. In highlighting the limits and unintended consequences of delivering constructivist accounts of nature, these new geographies can be drawn upon to re-assess the contribution of social constructivist approaches to childhood. Moreover, these relational accounts of nature gesture towards ways in which childhood scholars might reconceptualise the 'nature' of childhood without returning to the nature/culture divide.

Universality of Childhood

In an important paper in 2005, Qvortrup challenged the increasingly dominant focus within childhood studies on the plurality of childhoods, at the expense of focusing on the universality of childhood as a social category. According to James (2010), his critique centred on the argument that by focusing on the complexity and multiplicity of childhoods, the political power of the singular category of childhood, which lies in its ability to draw attention to the way in which children are marginalised and made invisible in social and economic policy, was being undermined and weakened:

> ... the promoters of the plurality thesis typically belong to the social constructionist mood or the post-modernist strands of social research with strong reservations against so-called grand narratives and generalisations and thus against what they see as unitary or even deterministic explanations. They have a strong sense for perceiving the society as complex and therefore for avoiding simple – or in their view simplistic – explanations, which at the end of the day typically leads to a preference for uniqueness. Each childhood, therefore, is a unique childhood with its particular points of reference which cannot fully be shared by others' childhoods. (Qvortrup, 2005)

Qvortrup's position suggests that, as childhood studies is not yet firmly enough established, the increasing emphasis on the plurality of childhoods was obscuring the overriding importance of childhood as a social category and its structural significance in terms of generation and intergenerational relations. By diverting attention away from generational relations, the project of childhood studies is somehow put at risk. This 'generational perspective' (Alanen, 2001) is another important dimension to explaining children and childhood. There are two aspects of the concept of generation which can be very helpful in studying childhood. The first aspect considers the different processes by which childhood is constructed and modified: in relationships between children and adults; in group transactions between teachers and pupils; and in relations between people born at different periods in history. The second aspect examines the extent to which children inhabit a generation, viewing themselves differently from older social groups. The ways in which children think of themselves can be seen as occupying a common generational location, one structured by adults' beliefs and behaviour (Mayall, 2002).

The concept of generational location is very helpful here because it turns our attention to the relational processes between adulthood and childhood, how adults use their positions of power to define differences between adults and children. It is the structural commonalities that define childhood as a separate generational space, where children are set aside from adults. At all levels of analysis (e.g. individual, group or cohort) in this generational approach, sociologists should focus on how children and adults negotiate decisions through space and time (Mayall, 2002). For example, at school, although rules are enforced and cultural assumptions deeply embedded, there is often some scope for modification by children through discussion and resistance.

Alanen (2009a) has further added to this generational perspective by introducing the concept of 'generational order'. This emphasises the power dimensions through which children and adults position themselves: the social position of children is produced and lived out by children as agents that are situated within other structural processes such as parenthood. An analysis of childhood must therefore be built around the structures and institutions of the particular society in which children live: childhood is situated within a system of social stratification and is part of a set of generational relations with older age groups – 'all children have parents in one form or another and are socialized in one way or another – the details will vary but the process is common' (James, 2010: 493).

Conclusions

In these concluding remarks, I want to summarise the different contributions that sociologists and historians have made to the sociology of childhood, suggesting a way of bringing these different areas together to develop a relational sociology of early childhood. There is no doubt that Philippe Ariès' influential book *Centuries of Childhood* (1962) inspired a wide range of historical studies that explored the emergence of various versions of childhood in earlier periods. But his claims for the uniqueness of childhood as a historical, Western European construction generated heated debates and critiques (see, for example, De Mause, 1991).

In a similar way to these polarised discussions about whether the history of childhood has distinct ruptures or overall continuities, sociologists of childhood have struggled to overcome a strong dichotomy between universal or multiple versions of childhood. The result has been a historical trajectory that 'zig-zags between the poles of the opposition, now placing childhood at the biological end, now the social' (Prout, 2005: 43–44). One important consequence is that the study of childhood has become the object of distinct fields of scientific study that do not communicate. As Thorne (2007: 150) writes, a 'wall of silence' stands in the way of dialogue between developmental psychology and the social sciences of childhood.

Alanen (2009b) has called for sociologists to develop a consistent sociology of childhood, one that incorporates the theoretical insights of the 'relational turn in sociology', offering the potential for interdisciplinary and cross-disciplinary collaboration. As I mentioned in my introductory chapter, a relational sociology of childhood can provide a more dynamic analysis of the structural relations of young children's lives, focusing on how young children see themselves in relation to their older counterparts, usually teachers and parents, though this should also include their relationships with peers and siblings. Alanen has suggested that Bourdieu's theoretical concepts of field, habitus and capital can be used to consider the particularity of childhood and its large-scale character and status (Alanen and Siisiainen, 2011) – this will be further discussed in more detail in Chapter 4.

Elias (2006) can also provide a very important way of developing interdisciplinary collaboration, providing a 'framework within which childhood can be seen as simultaneously part of culture and nature while not treating either as a distinct, autonomous or pure entity' (Prout, 2005: 3). He argues that we need to clearly define the difference and relationship between *biological evolution*, *social development* and *history*. These three concepts form distinct but inseparable layers in a process encompassing the whole of humanity, but each level runs at a different speed. In biological evolution, 10,000 years is a very short period. The changes that have taken place in the biological constitution of our species are relatively slight. Although there were some evolutionary changes in the social relationships of our ancestors, whether they were the Ancient Egyptians or the English, we are always concerned with human beings, people like ourselves: 'Whatever the ancestors of humanity may have been, as far as we can see back into the past we see an unbroken chain of parents and children, who in turn become parents' (Elias, 2010: 24).

However, in social development 10,000 years is a considerable period of time because the changes in social organisation that have taken place are relatively enormous. What makes history possible is that the structure of our social life takes place without changes in our biological constitution – historical change is possible because the experiences gathered from one generation need to be transmitted to the next. In every generation, young children need to learn from their elders and adults need to ensure the survival and care for biologically immature human beings, though the particular form of childhood is historically specific.

But in terms of the time it takes for young children to grow into old men and women, long-term social developments take place so slowly that they seem to stand still. This gives the impression that developments in the relationship between adults and young children are static, rather than structured changes in social expectations and behaviour. Passed on from one generation to the next, young children need to learn and internalise an enormous social fund of knowledge about the world.

In the next chapter, I will present the main theoretical argument for the sociology of early childhood, one that develops a flexible and dynamic approach that can understand the early years as a distinctive period of human development, integrating research findings on young children from a range of different, but related, disciplines like biology, psychology and history. Drawing on Norbert Elias's work, I will argue that it is crucial for sociologists to explain the different levels of biological and social processes in the development of young children.

DISCUSSION ACTIVITY

Interview two or three generations of your own family, identifying some of the major turning points or key events in their early childhood. In what ways are your own childhood experiences similar or different?

Further Reading

H. Hendrick (1997) *Children, Childhood and English Society, 1880–1990.* Cambridge: Cambridge University Press.

This book reviews the main findings of a number of historians on a range of topics including the changing social constructions of childhood, child-parent relations, social policy, schooling, leisure and the argument that modern childhood is 'disappearing'. Harry Hendrick is a very important British historian of childhood and this book had an enormous influence on my own thinking about the history of childhood.

A. James and A. Prout (eds) (1997) *Constructing and Reconstructing Childhood,* 2nd edition. London: Falmer.

Allison James and Alan Prout are two of the most important social scientists in the establishment of the new sociology of childhood. This classic text offers a range of articles by leading sociologists, historians, anthropologists, psychologists and child advocates.

W.L. Corsaro (2011) *The Sociology of Childhood*, 3rd edition. London: Sage.

Since its first publication in 1997, *The Sociology of Childhood* has been one of the major texts in the sociological study of children and childhood. Its main theoretical approach is 'interpretative reproduction', emphasising that children should be seen as participants with their own peer cultures, which influence and resist the adult world.

References

Alanen, L. (2001) 'Explorations in Generational Analysis', in L. Alanen and B. Mayall (eds), *Conceptualising Child-Adult Relations*. London: Routledge, pp. 11–22.

Alanen, L. (2009a) 'Generational Order', in J. Qvortrup, W.A. Corsaro and M.S. Honig (eds), *The Palgrave Handbook of Childhood Studies*. Basingstoke: Palgrave Macmillan, pp. 159–174.

Alanen, L. (2009b) 'Rethinking Childhood with Bourdieu', in A.M. Markstrom, M. Simonsson, I. Soderlind and E. Angard (eds), *Barn, Barndom och Foraldrarskap*. Stockholm: Carlssons, pp. 307–324.

Alanen, L. and Siisiainen, M. (eds) (2011) *Fields and Capitals: Constructing Local Life*. Jyvaskyla: Finnish Institute for Educational Research.

Alderson, P. and Morrow, V. (2011) *The Ethics of Research with Children and Young People: A Practical Handbook*. London: Sage.

Archer, T. (1870) *The Terrible Sights of London and Labours of Love in the Midst of Them*. London: Stanley Rivers and Co.

Ariès, P. (1962) *Centuries of Childhood*. London: Jonathan Cape.

Australian Senate Community Affairs References Committee (2001) *Lost Innocents: Righting the Record Report on Child Migration*. Canberra: Senate Printing Unit.

Buckingham, D. (2000) *After the Death of Childhood: Growing Up in the Age of Electronic Media*. Cambridge: Polity Press.

Carr, E.H. (1987) *What is History?*, 2nd edition. London: Penguin.

Cunningham, H. (1991) *The Children of the Poor: Representations of Childhood Since the Seventeenth Century*. Oxford: Blackwell.

Cunningham, H. (2005) *Children and Childhood in Western Society since 1500*. Harlow: Pearson Longman.

Deleuze, G. and Guattari, F. (1988) *A Thousand Plateaus*. Minneapolis: University of Minnesota Press.

De Mause, L. (1991) *The History of Childhood*. London: Bellew.

Drotner, K. and Livingstone, S. (2008) (eds) *The International Handbook of Children, Media and Culture*. London: Sage.

Elias, N. (2006) *The Court Society*. Dublin: UCD Press [Collected Works, vol. 2].

Elias, N. (2010) *The Society of Individuals*. Dublin: UCD Press [Collected Works, vol. 10].

Elkin, F. and Handel, G. (1972) *The Child and Society: The Process of Socialization*, 2nd edition. New York: Random House.

Ennew, J. and Watson, R. (2009) 'The Right to be Properly Researched: Research with Children in a Messy, Real World', *Children's Geographies*, 7(4): 365–378.

Frijhoff, W. (2012) 'Historian's Discovery of Childhood', *Paedagogica Historica: International Journal of the History of Education*, 48(1): 11–29.

Fuller, P. (1979) 'Uncovering Childhood', in M. Hoyles (ed.), *Changing Childhood*. London: Writers and Readers Publishing Co-operative, pp. 71–108.

Gombrich, E.H. (2008) *A Little History of the World*. New Haven, CT and London: Yale University Press.

Haraway, D. (2008) *When Species Meet*. Minneapolis: University of Minnesota Press.

Harrison, S., Pile, S. and Thrift, N. (eds) (2004) *Patterned Ground: Entanglements of Nature and Culture*. London: Reaktion Books.

Hart, R. (2007) *Children's Participation in Sustainable Development*. London: Earthscan.

Hendrick, H. (2003) *Child Welfare: Historical Dimensions, Contemporary Debate*. Bristol: Policy Press.

Heywood, C. (2010) 'Centuries of Childhood: An Anniversary and an Epitaph?', *The Journal of the History of Childhood and Youth*, 3(3): 341–365.

Holt, J.C. (1975) *Escape from Childhood: The Needs and Rights of Children*. Harmondsworth: Penguin.

Instone, L. (2004) 'Situating Nature: On Doing Cultural Geographies of Australian Nature', *Australian Geographer*, 35(2): 131–140.

James, A.L. (2010) 'Competition or Integration? The Next Step in Childhood Studies?', *Childhood*, 17(4): 485–499.

James, A. and James, A.L. (2004) *Constructing Childhood: Theory, Policy and Social Practice*. London: Palgrave Macmillan.

James, A. and Prout, A. (eds) (1997) 'Introduction', in *Constructing and Reconstructing Childhood*, 2nd edition. London: Falmer.

James, A., Jenks, C. and Prout, A. (1998) *Theorizing Childhood*. Cambridge: Polity.

Kline S. (1993) *Out of the Garden: Toys and Children's Culture in the Age of TV Marketing*. London: Verso.

Lange, A. and Mierendorff, J. (2009) 'Method and Methodology in Childhood Research', in J. Qvortrup, W. Corsaro and M. Honig (eds), *The Palgrave Handbook of Childhood Studies*. Basingstoke: Palgrave Macmillan, pp. 78–95.

Latour, B. (2005) *Reassembling the Social: An Introduction to Actor-Network Theory*. Oxford: Oxford University Press.

Lee, N. and Motzkau, J. (2011) 'Navigating the Bio-politics of Childhood', *Childhood*, 18(1): 7–19.

Marsh, J. (2010) *Childhood, Culture and Creativity: A Literature Review*. Newcastle: Creativity, Culture and Education Series.

Mayall, B. (2002) *Towards a Sociology for Childhood: Thinking from Children's Lives*. Buckingham: Open University.

Mayall, B. (2012) 'An Afterword: Some Reflections on a Seminar Series', *Children's Geographies*, 10(3): 347–355.

McMillan, M. (1930) *The Nursery School*. London: Dent.

McNamee, S. and Seymour, J. (2012) 'Towards a Sociology of 10–12 Year Olds? Emerging Methodological Issues in the "New" Social Studies of Childhood', *Childhood*, 20(2): 156–168.

Morrison, H. (ed.) (2012) *The Global History of Childhood Reader*. London: Routledge.

Motzkau, J.F. (2010) 'Speaking up Against Justice: Credibility, Suggestibility and Children's Memory on Trial', in J. Haaken and P. Reavey (eds), *Memory Matters: Contexts for Understanding Sexual Abuse Recollections*. London: Routledge, pp. 63–85.

Müller, A. (2009) *Framing Childhood in Eighteenth-Century English Periodicals and Prints, 1689–1789*. Farnham: Ashgate.

Opie, I. and Opie, P. (1959) *The Lore and Language of Schoolchildren*. Harmondsworth: Penguin.

Orme, N. (2001) *Medieval Childhood*. New Haven, CT and London: Yale University Press.

Palmer, S. (2006) *Toxic Childhood: How the Modern World is Damaging our Children and What We Can Do About It*. London: Orion Press.

Parsons, T. (1951) *The Social System*. Glencoe: Free Press.

Piaget, J. (1970) *Genetic Epistemology*. New York: Columbia University Press.

Pollock, L.A. (1983) *Forgotten Children: Parent-Child Relations from 1500 to 1900*. Cambridge: Cambridge University Press.

Prout, A. (2005) *The Future of Childhood*. London: RoutledgeFalmer.

Prout, A. (2011) 'Taking a Step Away from Modernity: Reconsidering the New Sociology of Childhood', *Global Studies of Childhood*, 1(1): 4–14.

Prout, A. and James, A. (1997) 'A New Paradigm for the Sociology of Childhood? Provenance, Promise and Problems', in A. James and A. Prout (eds), *Constructing and Reconstructing Childhood: Contemporary Issues in the Sociological Study of Childhood*, 2nd edition. London: Falmer, pp. 7–32.

Purdy, L.M. (1992) *In Their Best Interest? The Case Against Equal Rights for Children*. Ithaca, NY: Cornell University Press.

Qvortrup, J. (2005) 'The Little "s" and the Prospects for Generational Childhood Studies', Paper presented at the international conference, 'Childhoods 2005', Oslo, 29 June–3 July.

Richards, M.P.R. (1974) 'Introduction', in M.P.R. Richards (ed.), *The Integration of a Child into a Social World*. Cambridge: Cambridge University Press, pp. 1–10.

Shorter, E. (1977) *The Making of the Modern Family*. London: Fontana.

Smart, C., Neale, B. and Wade, A. (2001) *The Changing Experiences of Childhood – Families and Divorce*. Cambridge: Polity.

Stephens, S. (ed.) (1995) *Children and the Politics of Culture*. Princeton: Princeton University Press.

Stone, L. (1979) *The Family, Sex and Marriage in England, 1500–1800*, revised edition. London: Penguin.

Swain, S. (2009) 'Sweet Childhood Lost: Idealised Images of Childhood in the British Child Rescue Literature', *Journal of the History of Childhood and Youth*, 2(2): 198–214.

Taylor, A. (2011) 'Reconceptualizing the "Nature" of Childhood', *Childhood*, 18(4): 420–433.

Thompson, E.P. (1977) 'Happy Families', *New Society*, pp. 499–501.

Thomson, P. (2008) *Doing Visual Research with Children and Young People*. London: Routledge.

Thorne, B. (2007) Editorial: 'Crafting the Interdisciplinary Field of Childhood Studies', *Childhood*, 14(2): 147–152.

Tisdall, E.K.M., Davis, J.M. and Gallagher, M. (2009) *Research with Children and Young People: Research Design, Methods and Analysis*. London: Sage.

Tucker, E. (2008) *Children's Folklore: A Handbook*. Westport, CT: Greenwood Press.

Wells, K. (2009) *Childhood in Global Perspective*. Cambridge: Polity Press.

Wordsworth, W. (1888) T*he Complete Poetical Works*. London: Macmillan.

Wyness, M. (2006) *Childhood and Society: An Introduction to the Sociology of Childhood*, 2nd edition. Basingstoke: Palgrave Macmillan.

Zelizer, V.A. (1994) *Pricing the Priceless Child: The Changing Social Value of Children*. Princeton: Princeton University Press.

3

A RELATIONAL SOCIOLOGY OF EARLY CHILDHOOD

Introduction

This chapter will present the main theoretical argument for a relational sociology of early childhood, one that develops a flexible and dynamic approach that can understand and explain the early years as a distinctive period of human development, integrating research findings on young children from a range of different but related disciplines like biology, psychology and history. In the last chapter I discussed some of the recent concerns expressed by contemporary sociologists of childhood about the future direction of their area. James (2010), for example, argues that it has reached a crossroads in its development because of the competing paradigms that are now being pursued under the interdisciplinary umbrella of childhood studies. He believes that fault lines are beginning to emerge in what was once a unified project, reflecting tensions between key areas and theoretical positions.

For sociologists of childhood one of the most important debates has centred on the role of developmental psychology in explaining young children's lives – they have traditionally rejected most forms of 'developmentalism', especially those based on the Piagetian perspective, as a 'stage' and 'age' approach to young children's development. However, it is crucial to provide a more balanced assessment of the contribution of developmental theories of childhood by arguing that these critiques overstate their case, rejecting wide-ranging scholarship labelled under the broad heading 'child development' (Woodhead, 2008). When we begin to rethink the relation between biological and psychological approaches to young children's development, it is then possible to develop a more nuanced critique of a narrow 'developmentalism'.

We have recently celebrated some major anniversaries in our understanding of biological knowledge – the 150th anniversary of the publication of Charles Darwin's *On the Origin of Species*, the 60th anniversary of the discovery of the structure of DNA and the 10th anniversary of the deciphering of the human genome. However, many social scientists still have a monolithic notion of biology (Jackson and Rees, 2007), looking at this discipline from a distance rather than from an actual sense of how it is currently being explored with all its complexity, plurality and internal conflicts. Within theoretical biology there is an explosion of intellectual movements, such as Developmental Systems Theory (DST) (Oyama et al., 2001), Niche-Construction (Lewontin, 2001) and Evo-Devo (Müller, 2007), which are symptomatic of the very fluid status of evolutionary theory and the heated debate within it. Each of these new theories highlight certain shortcomings of the neo-Darwinian consensus: the flux of information is not only one-directional, from genes to organisms (DST); the organism is not a passive object of the environment but contributes to its construction (Niche-Construction); and development is not the mere activation of a 'genetic programme' that can be sidelined when understanding evolution (Evo-Devo) (Meloni, 2014).

For Rose (1997), these radical ideas are best captured by the concept of 'autopoiesis', which seeks to reconcile the organism and its life-line as a process of becoming, through which the living organism constructs itself. Rose's aim, along with others such as Jablonka and Lamb (2006) is to 'make biology whole again'. This new holistic biology emphasises the dynamic relationship between organisms and their environments:

> To put the organism and its lifeline back at the core of biology, to counter the gene's eye view of the world that has come to dominate much current popular and even technical philosophical writing on biology over the past two decades, means replacing the static, reductive, DNA-centred view of living systems with an emphasis on the dynamics of life. We need instead to be concerned with process, with the paradox of development by which any organism has simultaneously to *be* and *become*, as when a newborn infant must be capable of sucking at the breast while at the same time developing the competence to chew and digest solid food, and with the continuous interchange between organisms and their environments. (Rose, 1997: 18, italics in original)

Quilley (2010) argues that the re-emergence of holism in biology and the recognition of complexity is a significant development for sociologists for two reasons. Firstly, the imperialist explanatory logic of early socio-biology, which would reduce sociology to biology, has been undercut by developments *within* the life sciences. According to Meloni (2014), the epistemology of the life sciences has significantly changed over the last two decades, but many of these changes seem to remain unnoticed amongst sociologists: the majority who reject biology and the minority who want to biologise sociological theory share a common understanding of 'the biological' that appears increasingly out of date with recent advances in the bio-sciences. Secondly, within this recognition of new developments in the bio-sciences, there is space for sociology alongside genetics, ecology and a range of other disciplines to investigate the complexity of human life in societies.

The chapter will therefore argue that sociologists need to begin to stop rejecting biological knowledge, overcoming some of their deepest fears about biological reductionism and the role of developmental psychology. For Norbert Elias (2009) it was crucial for sociologists to determine the relation between nature, culture and society, and the unique characteristics that distinguish human beings from other animal species. He argued that one of the distinctive characteristics of the human species is the 'inter-locking' of biological and social processes in the development of young children. He coined the phrase 'love and learning' to draw attention to the way in which young children's development is both a cognitive and affective process, intimately woven together in different societies.

To develop a relational sociology of early childhood, we need to investigate the various lines of early child development by integrating research findings on young children from a range of different, but related, disciplines. Within developmental psychology there is a significant turn towards a relational psychology, a growing trend to criticise what has been termed the spectator theory of knowledge, where participants are required to merely observe others or think about their 'mental states' rather than participate in social interaction with them (see Reddy, 2008). A second person approach overcomes this 'spectatorial gap' by focusing on how it feels to engage with another person, where people are not isolated from others but embedded in the real world (Schilbach et al., 2013). Fogel et al. (2006) have also placed an emphasis on relationships which are relational and historical. First, the developing relationship, not the individual child, is the unit of analysis. Second, that change emerges from but is not entirely constrained by patterns of the past. Third, the developmental process is best revealed by making observations within a particular case before, during and after a key developmental transition.

The Biological and the Social

As I mentioned in the previous chapter, a key problem for sociologists of childhood was bio-social dualism: how do the biological and the social shape the growing child? As some sociologists of childhood have pointed out (Lee, 2001; Prout, 2005), the dominant psychological and sociological disciplinary perspectives are still predominantly polarised around an understanding of childhood as biological and hence natural, or as a social construct and hence cultural. This is most clearly illustrated in the popular nature/nurture debate, which is concerned not with questioning the categories of nature and nurture themselves, but in commentating upon their interactions or in ascertaining the relative proportions of culture's influence upon childhood and nature's determination of it.

Taylor (2011) suggests that within this field there is a degree of difference in emphasis and approach. Interrogations range from ones that point to tensions between interpretations over chronological age differences to those that refute all realist assumptions about childhood as a 'natural' life stage, by stressing its discursive construction. Hultqvist and Dahlberg (2001: 9), for example, have pointed to the 'historically produced discourses and power relations that constitute the child as an object and subject of knowledge, practice, and political intervention'.

Foucault's (2007) ideas about power focus on its ability to shape and form both the population as a collectivity and individual subjectivity, through the application of a range of techniques, or disciplines, including surveillance, normalisation, exclusion, classification and regulation. He explains the emergence of this new kind of 'disciplinary power' from the seventeenth century onwards, a power not concerned with sovereignty and the overt coercion of people, but with their management, organisation, orchestration and the shaping of conduct. On the basis of scientific credibility and techniques of disciplinary power new types of intervention are continually developed to control the relationships between young children and adults. From conception, children's lives become subject to monitoring and evaluation.

For Foucault (2007), the sphere of the state's strategic involvement in the life, growth and flourishing of their populations has long been a basic concern of governments. Moss and Petrie (2002) have argued that when young children increasingly becoming objects of central government policy we need more than ever to question our commonplace assumptions about childhood. Through the promotion of 'normalising' discourses, developmental psychology has played a key role in the scientific study of young children.

I now want to explore in greater depth the debate around developmentalism, 'the set of ideas about the child and childhood systematised and promulgated by child psychology' (Stainton Rogers and Stainton Rogers, 1992: 37), to illustrate one of the most important tensions in the bio-social approach. In the early twentieth century, developmental psychology became established as the dominant paradigm for studying young children, influencing professional practice in care and education (Woodhead, 2003). The study of child development offered insights into how best to intervene in the life of the child in order to promote children's future welfare. Discourses about ages and stages became linked to developmental norms, encoded in milestones and developmental delay. Within this framework, childhood is viewed as an apprenticeship for adulthood that can be charted through stages related to age, physical development and cognitive ability: groups of children were organised according to their birth dates, institutionalised in age-graded classrooms with their progress tracked according to predefined key stages (Woodhead, 2008).

Turmel (2008) provides an important and detailed historical account of three major phases, age structuration, stage and sequence in 'developmental thinking', paving the way for the central role that developmental psychology would play in the scientific study of children. Age structuration refers to age standards or age norms – in 1842, British physicians Evanson and Maunsell introduced a division of childhood into two categories: birth to age one and age one to age eight, dentition being the onset of the second phase. The transition from age categories into stages of development can be traced to physicians' clinical research and advice on natural growth. They articulated progressive age standards with growth phases as well as the specific circumstances surrounding children's diseases. For example, in a widely influential text of the 1890s, Starr (1894) collected data that indicated what should be the normal proportions, height and weight, of a child at each age. The final sequential phase came later in the 1920s, and enabled scientists to move from an extensive description of the child's physical condition to an understanding of his or her mental capability, mainly intelligence, epitomised in Piaget's (1927) developmental model, a structuring of thought through more and more complex stages.

Jenks (1996) and Morss (1990) have argued that the developmental approach in psychology that emerged in the nineteenth century was based on an evolutionary model that emphasised natural growth as a biological series of stages from childhood to adulthood. The origins of developmental psychology can be traced to seminal texts, among them Darwin's 1877 'A Biographical Sketch of an Infant', Wilhelm Preyer's

Die Seele des Kindes published in 1882 and G. Stanley Hall's 'Content of Children's Minds', published the following year (Archard, 2004). Morss' critique of developmentalism is based around the predominance of biological ideas in developmental thinking – according to him, young children's maturation is universally constructed as a sequence of progressive, developmental states, evolutionary in its framework. Central to the stage framework is linear progression and periodicity: each phase, stamped by regularity and repetition, must be completely gone through before reaching adulthood. The idea of progress is underpinned by evolutionary theory and is at the core of the concept of development.

According to Woodhead (2008), James et al. (1998) went furthest in their critique of traditional developmental psychology, focusing on the assumptions of one of the most influential developmental researchers in twentieth-century Europe, Jean Piaget. As immature learners, young children are viewed as a set of 'potentials', a 'project in the making', researched within an evaluative frame that is mainly interested in their position on the stage-marked journey to mature, rational, responsible, autonomous, adult competence. However Woodhead (2008) steers a balanced course and argues that although the rigidity of these developmental stages was rightly challenged, this should be viewed within the context of early twentieth-century public attitudes towards young children. Developmental approaches did not diminish the status of young children's thinking, but were used to reform social practices.

He argues that researching biological, social and cultural processes of human learning and development is consistent with an agenda for childhood studies, concluding that while 'Cruder versions of developmentalism may properly be consigned to the dustbin of history, it would be a mistake to discard a field as diverse as developmental psychology' (Woodhead, 2008: 28-29). He believes that concepts and tools are still needed that acknowledge children are, for the most part, relatively inexperienced members of society. They require guidance, support and teaching from more experienced social actors, through enabling structures and pedagogies for participation.

John Bowlby's Theory of Attachment

A human being is completely dependent on others for survival and it is years before the young child can meet his or her basic needs for food and shelter, manage to control overwhelming feelings in situations of stress or fear and recognise and avoid dangers. This process of attachment is so complex that staying near to a caregiver who will protect and sustain the child's life is crucial. But it can also be fraught with deep emotional uncertainty – Jeanette Winterson (2011) recalls in *Why Be Happy When You Could Be Normal?* how the painful past returned to haunt her life as she went in search of her real mother. Adopted by Pentecostal parents in a northern town in England, she writes with irony about her strict religious upbringing:

> Until I was two years old, I screamed. This was evidence in plain sight that I was possessed by the Devil. Child psychology hadn't reached Accrington, and in spite of important work by Winnicott, Bowlby and Balint on attachment, and the trauma of early separation from the love object that is the mother, a screaming baby wasn't a broken-hearted baby – she was a Devil baby. (Winterson, 2011: 20)

An important aspect of Bowlby's attachment theory is its focus on the biological roots of attachment. During the time when humans were evolving, genetic selection favoured attachment behaviours that increased the likelihood of child–mother proximity, which increased protection and survival. Bowlby (1969) argued that there is an attachment behaviour system which is specific to human beings and leads to important benefits that result from the young child's proximity to the parent, including feeding, learning about the environment and social interaction.

But the most important survival advantage to the child is protection from predators. Infants who were more biologically predisposed to stay close to their mothers were less likely to be killed by predators. This is known as the biological function of attachment behaviour: without protection from predators, feeding and learning cannot take place. Bowlby concluded that all young children need to have a warm, intimate and continuous relationship with their mother or a permanent mother substitute. Moreover, he believed that there is a sensitive period for this relationship to develop, from six to 30 months. If the relationship is absent or broken, the consequences are severe and irreversible: the young child will grow up affectionless, unable to form close relationships with others.

This crucial concept of a critical period had its origins in ethology. Ethologists provide a biological framework for studies of social behaviour by emphasising techniques of observation of animals in their natural habitat. An ethological approach appealed to Bowlby because of its roots in 'naturalistic' observation and because it also provided a theoretical critique of psychoanalysis. According to Holmes (1993: 132), 'attachment theory is perhaps seen as a variant of object-relations theory': Freud's theory of instincts and drives is replaced by an assumption that humans are fundamentally relation-seeking creatures. In the traditional psychoanalytic view, human beings are driven by instinctual drives; in contrast, in object-relations theory, the organism is not an isolated drive-driven creature in search of an instinctual object but a person relating to other persons.

Bowlby was particularly attracted to the systematic observation and application of research methods derived from the European School of animal behaviour studies headed by Lorenz and Tinbergen. Lorenz's theory (1957 [1935]) on imprinting in graylag geese was of particular interest to him, because it showed that in some species of bird, strong bonds to an individual mother figure could develop without any reference to food. Imprinting is a rapid form of learning in which familiarity with the specific characteristics of the mother hen are learned in a few hours after hatching by the baby chick. This early experience of following the mother allowed geese to bond without feeding by learning the specific visual characteristics of the mother.

He applied this ethological approach to compare the different mechanisms involved in early parent–child relationships, focusing on some of the important differences between species, but also on some of the similarities in closely related primates. He was influenced by Harlow et al.'s (1963) experimental studies that suggested that in the rearing of rhesus monkeys the infant's attachment behaviours (clasping and clinging) lead to close proximity and contact more often with a cloth mother surrogate that is soft than with another which gives milk. Although the first attachment bond in humans is analogous to these monkeys, Bowlby argued that it is based on species-specific human behaviours. In human infants, because clinging is so poorly developed, crying and smiling become even more crucial for eliciting maternal caretaking in the early months. He therefore contended that the attachment system is not related to feeding or the by-product of fundamental drive processes proposed within the psychoanalytic tradition.

'Sensitive' or 'Critical' Periods

However, the idea of a sensitive or critical period is not without controversy. Bruer (2013) argues that the notion of a critical or sensitive period can easily lead to 'The Myth of the First Three Years', which he states as follows. The age from birth to three is the period of peak synaptic density (that is the peak number of synapses per volume of brain tissue) in the human brain, during which more synapses form than are eliminated. Synaptic densities peak during early childhood at levels exceeding adult densities. The dramatic changes in the growth peaks of different components of the brain and the maturation of structures and processes that depend on them mean that there are sensitive periods when an enriched environment is more likely to support young children's development (Walker et al., 2011). These sensitive phases of development draw our attention to the way in which important areas of development have to be 'stimulated', 'activated' and patterned by social relationships if they are to develop.

However, Bruer argues that the myth of development in the early years relies on a narrow, rigid notion of a critical period, where the 'windows of opportunity slam shut' never to be opened again. He believes it is not the case that birth to three is *the* critical period for brain development. First, even for a single system like vision, each function – acuity, colour vision, motion vision, depth perception, binocular vision – has its own sensitive period, some stretching into the teenage years. Evolution has resulted in neural systems that *expect* to encounter certain kinds of stimuli in the environment in order to fine-tune their performance. Second, the sensitive periods we do know about do not all happen during the first three years of life. Rutter (2002) argues that a distinction needs to be made between developmentally constrained critical periods versus life-long learning because these periods constrain only limited kinds of development.

Nevertheless, it is important to emphasise that Bowlby was trying to steer a middle course between learning approaches that are solely dependent on learnt behaviour, excluding any 'built-in social responses', yet at the same time avoiding a return to a naive version of biological determinism. For Bowlby (1979: 40), crying, sucking and smiling are good examples of how the balance in the biological equipment of the newborn child 'has tipped far in favour of flexibility of behaviour, and therefore of learning, and away from in-built fixity'. Smiling is a good illustration of the way the evolutionary process has facilitated young human beings to live in groups, 'to convey to others a rich variety of shades of feeling' (Elias, 2009: 157). In human infants, eye contact with adults leads to their smiling between eight weeks and three months and continues as the infant is growing.

Fogel et al. (2006) discovered context-specific nuances in infant smiles during the second half of the first year of their lives. They investigated different types of smiles during two mother–infant games – peekaboo and tickle – at six and 12 months. Rather than a single smile expression that differs only in how wide the smile is (amplitude), they found a complex range of smile expressions that are different in their duration and amplitude. As active learners, babies were able to control the type and amplitude of their smiling in response to the playing of the game, the set-up (anticipation of the fun to come) and its climax.

Although Bowlby drew attention to smiling and to the behavioural equipment of the human neonate (see, in particular, Bowlby, 1969: 268–296), it is important to ask to what extent he eventually returned to a form of biological reductionism. He gives a good example (Bowlby, 1969: 61–62) where, although he acknowledges that there are differences between 'man and sub-human species', 'their similarities are equally important, and perhaps more so than their differences'. Later in his book on attachment, in a sub-section entitled 'Differences from and similarities with that seen in sub-human primates', one would expect from the title some differences to be mentioned in attachment behaviour. But once again, although he points to the mother keeping in close contact with human infants, because they are less mobile than other primates, he is nevertheless keen to downplay these differences: 'Thus the difference in infant–mother relations in gorilla and in man is not so great' (Bowlby, 1969: 198–199).

Biological Reductionism

Edwards et al. (2014) have forcefully criticised what they see as the 'biologised conception of children's future potential'. They argue that the embellishment of the early intervention evidence base within brain science has led to mothers being blamed for their inadequate parenting. In British government commissioned reviews such as the Independent Review on Poverty and Life Chances (Field, 2010), it is claimed that cycles of deprivation can be broken by teaching poor mothers how to love their babies more effectively. According to Edwards et al. (2014), this increasingly gendered policy emphasises the centrality of mother–child relationships by referring to a child's biological need for an available and responsive primary caregiver.

Burman (2008) has similar concerns that attachment theorists and, more generally, developmental psychologists, in their attempt to overcome the division between the biological and the social by referring to the 'adaptedness' of the infant for social interaction, present an impoverished view of what it means to be social. The social is primarily represented by the mother–child relationship, which is further equated with communication and then finally seen as 'interpersonal'. Burman argued that developmental psychologists like Bowlby lapse into a form of biological reductionism by dissolving the social into the biological, ignoring other significant relationships that involve infants and young children. In the attempt to overcome the division between the 'social' and the 'cultural', an evolutionary perspective once again is reintroduced, one that fragments 'cultural variation into individual differences' (Burman, 2008: 55).

Burman, however, is herself in danger of reproducing the divisions between 'biology' and 'society' and 'nature' and 'culture' by placing too much emphasis on the socially constructed aspects of child development. Wood (2007) has developed a more nuanced approach by arguing that it is mistaken to assume that evolutionary psychology must necessarily be deterministic or reductive. Rogoff (2003) is a good example of one such approach. She criticises the idea of an innate maternal attachment, calling for a more contextualised model of biological and cultural processes. She warns against attributing neglect and abuse to failures in early maternal bonding rather than considering societal features and support for infant care.

The British psychoanalyst Winnicott has also challenged this idea of a 'perfect mother'. He strongly believed that an important part of a mother's role is to allow her infant to experience tolerable frustrations: a mother was not doing the best for her child if her aim was to alleviate all distress, discomfort and frustration at the earliest possible opportunity (Oates et al., 2005). Winnicott (1964) used the concept of the 'good-enough mother' to describe a mother who allows just the right amount of delay in meeting an infant's needs to encourage tolerance of waiting and confidence in ultimate satisfaction.

Attachment Patterns

These debates raise a central question – to what extent is attachment a universal function mainly carried out by mothers? Or is there a reper-toire of attachment patterns that are dependent on the different ways that young children are cared for around the world? In reviewing the literature on attachment relationships beyond the traditional mother–child dyad, Howes (1999) states that the key determinants for whether a young child forms a bond with non-maternal caregivers include:

1. Whether the caregiver provides both physical and emotional care
2. Whether that person is a consistent presence within the child's social network
3. Whether the caregiver has an emotional investment in the child.

Tizard (2009) forcefully argues that what is much less widely known is that Bowlby considerably developed and modified his theories over his lifetime, driven by a desire to be more scientific in his approach and to incorporate the concepts, methods and findings of other disciplines. He came to the conclusion that there is nothing sacrosanct about ongoing care being provided by the biological parents as long as it is able to be provided by other consistently and reliably available people. Indeed, he argued that a variety of attachment figures would encompass relations with different people, better preparing the young child for forming relationships with a wide range of people later in life.

In the context of care not provided by the members of the family, Howes points out that there is greater predictability in the pattern of interaction when a caregiver is consistently present for longer periods of time. Similarly Langston (2006: 9) emphasises that the importance to a young child of 'a second or subsidiary positive relationship cannot be overstated'. Although Bowlby believed that healthy attachment in infants is based on relatively long-term, stable relationships with carers, he did not see a single attachment with a mother (monotropy) as necessarily being the best and only way of achieving this. He also recognised that attachment to a father can support an infant's attachment to their mother and that other people in an infant's life can play important roles. Grossmann et al. (2002) found that children who excel in social situations as young adults had mothers who provided an enduring secure base and fathers who provided sensitive and exciting play activities. There seem to be two attachment roles for two significant functions – one attachment role is to provide love and security, the other to engage in exciting and challenging experiences (NICHD Early Childcare Research Network, 2004).

Richard Bowlby, the son of John Bowlby, suggested in an interview (Newland and Coyl, 2010) that fathers should be seen as the 'primary' attachment figure, which would help to re-evaluate the importance of a father's role. In families where there are two people raising young children, one parent could be the most important for providing an enduring secure base and haven of safety in times of distress, whilst the other parent could be the most important for providing exploration and excitement when times are favourable – different roles but equally significant. There will be varying degrees of overlap between these two attachment roles, but each parent will usually provide mostly one or the other type of attachment relationship. Fathers would then see themselves as having a crucial influence on their young children's long-term social development and their position as trusted play companions would, instead of so often being ridiculed as juvenile and time wasting, be highly valued.

To understand how attachment patterns can have a lasting influence, John Bowlby introduced the important concept of 'internal working models':

From the end of the first year, children are increasingly able to represent the world in symbolic form – they can think about their attachment figures, about themselves and about the relationship between themselves and the other person:

> The model of himself that he builds reflects also the images that his parents have of him, images that are communicated not only by how each treats him but by what each *says* to him. These models then govern how he feels towards each parent and about himself, how he expects each of them to treat him, and how he plans his own behaviour towards them. (Bowlby, 2005: 146, italics in original)

According to Schaffer (2004), these models emphasise that attachment is a lifelong process: they are representations of the past, but can also be used to guide behaviour in future close relationships. Bowlby believed that such models, built up by young children from their experiences and from what they are told, consist of expectations about how people will respond to them, and they to others. At first the models, whether based on negative or positive experiences, are tentative, but they tend to persist. Therefore any initial emotional damage to young children tends to be perpetuated, although to some extent it may be moderated by later experiences. Tizard (2009) makes a significant observation when she suggests that the concept of internal working models led Bowlby to withdraw his initial belief in a critical period for bonding. In the conclusion I discuss the important implications of this suggestion for the continuity of attachment bonds as young children grow up in society.

Love and Learning Relationships

For Norbert Elias (2009), it was crucial for sociologists to determine the relation between nature, culture and society and the unique characteristics that distinguish human beings from other animal species. As mentioned in the previous chapter, he made an important conceptual distinction between the term 'evolution', which refers to biological processes that are genetic and largely irreversible, and social 'development', processes which are malleable and potentially subject to change. In the evolutionary process, the biological propensity for learning is one of the main differences between animal and human societies, providing a framework for social development to take place without any biological changes. To identify the universal features of social life that make society possible, the adaptation of a distinctive biological organisation of human beings for learning needs to be understood. In terms of social-evolutionary development, the distinguishing, evolutionary breakthrough for human beings was that learned ways of steering behaviour became dominant in relation to unlearned forms.

One important issue in the development of young children is the relation between the biological basis of behaviour and the social conditions in which this activity takes place. For young children there are 'natural human structures which remain dispositions and cannot fully function unless they are stimulated by a person's "love and learning" relationship with other persons' (Elias, 2009: 147). The important relational concept of love and learning aptly summarises a great deal of previous psychological research on young children's development, bringing together specialised areas within psychology (particularly the separation between cognitive, social and developmental psychology).

In the following discussion, the relation between love and learning will be used as a sensitising concept to focus on the way in which young children's development is both a cognitive and affective process, one in which biological and social processes are intimately woven together in different types of societies. This draws attention to the relational turn in psychology and other related areas like relational pedagogy and education. I will also use the relation between love and learning as a framework to explore the significance of group processes in young children's relationships, moving beyond the individualistic emphasis given in attachment theory to the carer and young child. Bowlby's theory did not fully address the influence of multiple and simultaneous relationships experienced by infants and young children with other significant people in their lives (Lewis, 2005). What is particularly significant is the role that siblings and peer relationships play in the formation of young children's socio-emotional development.

Relational Bonds

The work of Colwyn Trevarthen (2005) is a good starting point for developing this relational approach to young children's development because he synthesises a great deal of recent neurological, biological and psychological research to highlight the unique biological equipment of human beings that prepares babies, infants and young children to enjoy and share companionship with others. Trevarthen (2005: 60–61) emphasises how the 'human body and brain' are adapted for communication: momentary shifts of gaze and 'gazing reverie' are made possible by the distinctive white sclera of human eyes and the versatility of human vocalisation achieved by the 'uniquely adapted human respiratory system'. Moving selves regulate contact with one another by 'felt immediacy' (Bråten, 2009), with emotions that direct an awareness of one another with different degrees of intimacy. The development of a young child's emotional health and future well-being in society depends on these unique human gifts for interpersonal life and sympathetic emotions (Trevarthen, 2011).

Faircloth's (2011) article is particularly illuminating here because she has attempted to move beyond the traditional divisions between the mind and body by exploring the relational bonds between mothers and young children. Through close attention to women's narratives of attachment parenting and 'full-term' breastfeeding, she has argued that a theoretical framework of 'affect' provides a more appropriate way of analysing women's accounts of breastfeeding than explanations which rely on 'hormones', 'instinct' or 'intuition', each of which is limited through a reductive logic that pays insufficient attention to the intensity and multifaceted nature of 'feeling' that women experience. Significantly, she considers 'affect' as a necessarily relational, bodily condition that incorporates the physiological and moral aspects of women's perceptions of themselves as mothers – 'doing what feels right in my heart'. It is a symbiotic process, involving the comfort that *both* mother and child receive in the process of breastfeeding: in their self-perception many of the mothers she interviewed talked about their experiences as a mutual endeavour, which was particularly poignant in the pre-verbal stage.

Reddy (2011) has adopted a relational framework to suggest that an understanding of joint attention between infants and carers should be seen as an embodied and relational process. She has argued that the affective charge of experiencing another person's attention underpins the later expansion of awareness of people's attention to objects which are beyond immediate reach: the infant's attention is focused neither on an object or another person, but on the relationship between the person and object. Another person's attention is not *discovered* late in infancy, but experienced by the infant as she feels the other person attending to her. This perspective can best be illustrated by what it feels like to see someone smiling at someone else and what it feels like when you notice that someone is smiling at you.

Until recently, the study of developmental psychology has been dominated by models of learning which have used the 'third-person perspective', standing apart from interactions and observing them from the outside (Reddy, 2008). Parker-Rees (2014) argues that in their concern to manage and control variables psychologists have driven the study of early interactions into clinic and baby labs – as a result, we now know more about how infants and caregivers behave in unfamiliar situations than how they behave in the privacy of their own homes where they are more likely to feel relaxed and comfortable. According to Bronfenbrenner (1979), more ecologically valid research with young children must fulfil three conditions – it should: (1) maintain the integrity of the real-life situations it is designed to investigate; (2) be faithful to the larger social and cultural contexts from which the subjects come; (3) be consistent with the participants' definition of the situation.

In the development of a more ecological approach, a key concept is the cultural-ecological niche (Super and Harkness, 1982: 48–49). For Valsiner (2000) this concept of a niche draws attention to the culturally important process of intergenerational continuity, where adults highlight particular aspects of development. This process, which he refers to as 'cultural highlighting', can take different forms – first, the high social value placed on some aspect of child development – for example, in Western societies the first steps of an infant walking independently are usually commented on by parents, relatives and friends. Second, there is an exaggeration of the symbolic importance of some particular developmental process. In mainstream developmental psychology the segregation of young children into similar-age groups, separating them from adults and older children, is taken for granted and not viewed as a specific cultural approach to raising children (Rogoff, 2003). This narrow focus of research is often based on middle-class European and American children spending a large portion of their day in age-segregated institutions such as institutional day care and schooling. Its research findings are often generalised to other communities without considering their cultural practices (LeVine and Norman, 2008), which may include young children learning from a wide range of activities in their communities (Rogoff et al., 2003).

Third, cultural highlighting may use negative stigmatisation of some aspect of development – for example, in Western societies there are pressures on women to breastfeed. For a range of immunological and nutritive reasons, the World Health Organization (2003) states that breastfeeding in developed countries should be exclusive for six months and continue 'for up to two years, or beyond' in conjunction with other foods. Because of its vital importance for the survival and healthy development of infants, feeding is a highly scrutinised domain where mothers must counter any charges of practising unusual, harmful or morally suspect feeding techniques (Murphy, 1999). Strong feelings about feeding are derived from the fact that it operates as a 'signal issue', over which women are placed into different parenting 'camps' (Kukla, 2005). The moralisation of infant-feeding decisions in a child-centred culture means that women's choices around feeding have become highly associated with maternal identity (Lee, 2007). In a culture where 'breast is best,' Murphy's work (1999: 187–188) with mothers who use formula milk in the early months addresses the moral work a woman has to undertake, if, as she puts it, she is to respond to the charge of being a 'poor mother' who places her own needs, preferences and convenience above her baby's welfare.

The fourth form of cultural highlighting concerns the cultural silences about certain aspects of development which are too dangerous for adults to discuss in front of their young children – this important area will later be discussed in Chapter 7, where we explore in greater depth parental concerns about the sexualisation of childhood and the role of the media.

Widening Group Processes

In a similar way to this relational and cultural turn in developmental psychology, there have been developments in relational pedagogy, understood as a complex web of human experiences rather than an individual experience divorced from its context. Papatheodorou (2009) argues that this signals a significant change in the conceptualisation of early years practice, bridging polarised discourses such as child-centred versus adult-centred learning. This also echoes Bronfenbrenner's (1979) argument that learning and development are related and determined by the dynamic interrelationships within and between four mutually inclusive systems: micro, meso, exo and macro. He mapped the different social contexts that affect development with his *bio-ecological model* of development. Bronfenbrenner's dynamic model allows us to see the relational connections between the different contextual layers that influence young children's development in different societies.

The *bio* aspect of the model emphasises that in their development young children are influenced by biological processes. The *ecological* refers to the social contexts in which they develop. Every child develops within a *microsystem* of his or her immediate relationships - close family, friends and teachers. This is the child's own 'little world' which is directly experienced. Within it relationships are reciprocal – they flow in both directions.

Microsystems exist within a *mesosystem*, which comprises the interrelations among two or more settings in which the young child actively participates, such as the relations between home, school or neighbourhood peer group. The mesosystem also interacts with the *exosystem*, another layer which includes all the social settings that affect the child, even though the child is not a direct member of the system. Examples are teachers' relations with school managers; parents' jobs; the community's resources for health, employment or recreation; or the family's religious affiliation. The *macrosystem* is the wider society – its values, laws, conventions and traditions, all of which influence the conditions and experiences of the young child's life. Bronfenbrenner (1979) emphasised that the belief systems or ideologies within a hierarchical macrosystem unify the other three systems because of their shared cultural values – for example, although nurseries in the UK may be different from one another, they still share similarities compared to nursery settings in other countries.

Writing about these pedagogical matters more than 80 years ago, the Scottish philosopher John Macmurray insisted that we should educate the emotions, placing relationships and care at the heart of teaching and learning. We are, in Macmurray's view, deeply and irrevocably relational beings whose creative energies are best realised in and through our encounters with others: he insists on education as a relational, caring undertaking:

> A child is born human; … He can survive only by being cared for. He can do nothing - just nothing - to help himself. He has to learn everything - to see, to move about, to walk, to speak: and while he is learning these basic elements of humanity, his human life consists in his relation to those who care for him - who feel for him, think and plan for him, act for him. This dependence on others is his life - yet to be human he must reach beyond it, not to independence, but to an *interdependence* in which he can give as well as receive. (Macmurray, 2012: 666–667, author's emphasis)

The work of Judy Dunn (1993) has been particularly important in broadening the theoretical frames through which young children's close relationships are researched. Although she recognises that attachment theorists have illuminated certain aspects of parent–child relationships and their significance in later life, the typology of the model they use is limited. In addition to a narrow view regarding the person with whom the infant interacts, the early research on attachment used a restricted definition of attachment, one that neglected other relevant aspects of relationships that affect quality, including, for example, humour and shared intimacy (Dunn, 1993: 114).

In a similar way Lewis (2005: 6) has argued that the attachment model is limited because it has led to 'a deterministic view of attachment in the literature and a serious restriction on attachment research itself'. A major assumption within the model is that there develops a linear relation such that the young child adapts to one relationship, and from this one relationship all subsequent ones follow. He suggests broadening attachment theory to make it more compatible with social network theory, which focuses on the family and wider community networks that infants and young children are born into. It is within this changing array of people and institutions that young children learn about the memberships rules of various networks. Parents, siblings, friends, childcare providers and educators all influence young children's social understanding and relationships.

In *Children's Friendships: The Beginnings of Intimacy* Dunn (2004) discusses the psychological aspects of young children's friendships, defining friendship as voluntary, reciprocal and mutually affectionate relationships where two people share their feelings and ideas. Friendship amongst infants begins as young as eight months old and from that time plays an integral role in young children's learning and involvement in daily routines and activities. One of the key differences between adult and child relationships and child–child relationships is the ability of same-age friends to engage in sustained dramatic play that is complex and harmonious: the mutuality of learning opportunities between siblings benefits both older and younger children as they play together, repeating, imitating, listening, echoing and challenging. Older children learn through practising what they know and translate official meanings into a personal sense for the younger child (Gregory, 2001). In an observational study of the social conversations of 43 children aged four years (Cutting and Dunn, 2006), the connections between young children's social cognition skills and their successful communication with both siblings and friends was noted. For the development of social relationships young children need to have the opportunity to engage in cooperative conversation and play.

This broadening of attachment theory to understanding peer relationships amongst young children should also be integrated with theories of development that take into consideration the context of different cultural communities, which are dynamic and often based on ethnic identity. Howes (2011) has argued that a suitable theoretical framework needs to take into account young children's home community as well as the history of relationships within their peer groups. Institutional settings for peer interaction contain individual children, dyads (child–caregiver, peer–peer friendships and playmates), and the group interaction between young children and their caregivers, as well as the tone the caregivers set for the entire setting. In contemporary societies, these all contribute to the social and emotional climate of the early childhood programmes where young children spend most of their time. One of the strengths of Howe's approach is that it helps to focus on the relational complexity of young children's experiences at these different levels: attention needs to be given to how individual children are situated within peer groups *and* to how these groups are nested within and across cultural communities.

Conclusions

This chapter has argued that to develop a suitable theoretical approach for a sociology of early childhood, sociologists need to overcome some of their deeply held suspicions about the role of biology in the historical development of human beings. While there are a small number of counter-examples, scholars in the mainstream social sciences work to keep biology *out* of their domain – to ward off the 'appalling appeal of nature' (Jackson and Rees, 2007). Fitzgerald et al. (2014) have argued that these efforts were understandable in the past because an early enthusiasm for biological ideas in the social sciences was deeply entangled in beliefs that human beings had a fixed 'essential' nature derived from evolution. However, in the twenty-first century they suggest that such suspicion is now unwarranted and prevents social scientists from exploring the important implications of contemporary developments in the social sciences. I have argued that in the place of these artificial barriers that have been constructed to prevent biologists, sociologists and psychologists from working together, we need a flexible and relational approach, capable of investigating the various aspects of young children's development.

I focused on John Bowlby's theory of attachment to highlight some of the weaknesses and strengths in constructing a theoretical framework that attempts to integrate the different social and biological levels in the early years of a child's life. Bowlby and Elias were both keen to investigate the emotional interdependencies that enabled infants and young children to survive, to grow up safe and secure in their societies. Important points of connection can be made between Elias's concept of 'open valencies', which emphasises the strong, affective ties that link people with one another, and the biological theory of attachment proposed by Bowlby: the behaviour of the young child and the stimulations he or she receives from parents (eye contact, smiles, vocal signals of affection) are considered important biological foundations for human relationships and for the building of emotional strength and security. Young children need consistent, sensitive and responsive loving care. A sensitive and responsive caregiver is one who sees the world from the young child's point of view and seeks to meet the child's needs rather than just serving their own. Growing up, young children use these early attachments to form relationships with other people in society.

I then discussed the influence of Lorenz's ethological theory on Bowlby's theory of attachment by responding to the important criticisms that it is too deterministic, reducing social relationships to biology. One of the key issues is the extent to which there is a sensitive or critical period, from six to 30 months, for a warm and intimate relationship between the mother and child to develop. Tizard (2009) claims that Bowlby modified his original view on attachment, integrating other perspectives from different disciplines such as information science – according to her, this led him to introduce the concept of internal working models, thus withdrawing his initial belief in a critical period for bonding. Although working models may show some continuity in content over time, their structure is likely to evolve substantially from infancy to childhood and adulthood. Young children's working models are likely to include simple information about caregivers' availability and responsiveness, whereas older children will incorporate more advanced cognitive processes such as imagining the partner's responses (Bretherton, 1990). McConnell and Moss' (2011) review of the factors that influence stability and change in attachment from infancy to adulthood significantly concluded that it is not only the quality of caregiving which is important during early childhood, but the role of the environment.

The way in which we begin to understand and explain young children's relationships within the 'environment' therefore becomes a crucial concern for sociologists of early childhood. I emphasised that Elias's concept of 'love and learning relationships' is very helpful, enabling us to focus on the relational turn that is beginning to emerge in other disciplines apart from sociology, particularly in psychology and early years' education. It also allows us to move beyond the exclusive focus on the mother–child relationship in early childhood which has hindered the opportunity to discuss the importance of sibling relationships and the value of early peer friendships for young children.

Within a new relational perspective, young children should be considered within the complexities of their families and in the increasing institutional arrangements now provided for babies and young children across many different parts of the world. Rossetti-Ferreira et al. (2011) offer a good example of this changing institutional context, focusing on peer relationships between babies, toddlers and pre-school age children in Brazilian day care centres. In a research programme that investigated the conditions that either favour or hinder babies and young children's interactions, they proposed that the exclusive focus on the mother–child dyad needs to be enlarged to include the socio-cultural context. It became clear to members of the research group that group settings for young children were different from the family environment and required new skills and knowledge which are distinct from mother-substitute care. They argued that caregivers share with families the care and education of their children, structuring routines for the more autonomous activities of young children. Opportunities for early peer interaction were mediated by a well-organised use of space which can be achieved using various materials, different textures, constructing tunnels or huts, or digging little channels where water can flow. In the next chapter I will further develop the theoretical approach for a sociology of early childhood, exploring the broader social processes that structure the institutional contexts within which young children grow up.

DISCUSSION ACTIVITY

Read carefully the following quotation from the sociologist Norbert Elias's *The Society of Individuals*.

But what we have here characterised as 'interweaving' to denote the whole relationship of individual and society can never be understood as long as 'society' is imagined, as is so often the case, essentially as a society of 'finished' individuals who were never children and never die. One can only gain a clear understanding of the relation of individual and society if one includes in it the perpetual maturation of individuals within a society, if one includes the process of individualisation in the theory of society. The historicity of each individual, the phenomenon of growing up to adulthood, is the key to understanding what 'society' is. The sociality integral to human beings only becomes apparent if one is aware what relations to other people mean for the small child. (Elias, 2010: 28–29)

Consider the following questions:

1. Why does Elias place so much emphasis on 'growing up to adulthood'?
2. As young children are growing up what kind of relationships are they developing?
3. Can you understand a society better by looking through a young child's eyes?

Further Reading

J. Dunn (2004) *Children's Friendships: The Beginnings of Intimacy.* Oxford: Blackwell.

Using real-life illustrations from her own studies as well as rich insights from novelists and biographers, Judy Dunn, one of the leading scholars of young children's development, brings alive the excitement, pleasures, problems and humour of young children's friendships. She draws on close observations of toddlers, pre-schoolers and school children to demonstrate the role of intimate friendships in encouraging children to share ideas, coordinate pretend play and express affection for those that are not kin.

Ian McIntosh and Samantha Punch (2009) '"Barter", "Deals", "Bribes" and "Threats": Exploring Sibling Interactions', *Childhood*, 16(1): 49–65.

A thought-provoking article that challenges the dominant psychological perspectives on siblings. Although the authors conducted interviews from a wider age group than the early years, their findings emphasise the importance of social context and children's own understandings of the sibling order. The dynamic nature of birth order position and age was a key finding: siblings engaged in forms of strategic interaction characterised both by a degree of calculation and self-interest as well as understandings of reciprocity, equivalence and fairness in their dealings with brothers and sisters.

Jeanette Winterson (2011) *Why Be Happy When You Could Be Normal?* London: Jonathan Cape.

This is a very engaging and at times humorous book that offers another perspective on a young child's upbringing. According to Winterson it was written in 'real time', 'When I began this book I had no idea how it would turn out. I was writing in real time. I was writing the past and discovering the future' (p. 226). This is evident from the book's structure, in which free-associative musings on religion, industrialisation, supermarkets and poetry are subtlety woven together by a deeply emotional narrative of how she tracked down her birth-mother through the adopted children register.

References

Archard, D. (2004) *Children: Rights and Childhood*, 2nd edition. London: Routledge.

Bowlby, J. (1969) *Attachment and Loss. Vol. 1, Attachment.* London: Hogarth Press.

Bowlby, J. (1979) *The Making and Breaking of Affectional Bonds.* London: Tavistock.

Bowlby, J. (2005) *A Secure Base.* London: Routledge.

Bråten, S. (2009) *The Intersubjective Mirror in Infant Learning and Evolution of Speech.* Amsterdam/Philadelphia: John Benjamins Publishing Company.

Bretherton, I. (1990) 'Open Communication and Internal Working Models: Their Role in Attachment Relationships', in R. Thompson (ed.), *Nebraska Symposium on Motivation. Vol. 36, Socioemotional Development.* Lincoln, NE: University of Nebraska Press, pp. 57–113.

Bronfenbrenner, U. (1979) *The Ecology of Human Development.* Cambridge, MA: Harvard University Press.

Bruer, J.T. (2013) *Revisiting 'The Myth of the First Three Years'*. Centre for Parenting Culture Studies, University of Kent. Available at: http://blogs.kent.ac.uk/parentingculturestudies/files/2011/09/Special-briefing-on-The-Myth.pdf

Burman, E. (2008) *Deconstructing Developmental Psychology*, 2nd edition. London: Routledge.

Cutting, A.L. and Dunn, J. (2006) 'Conversations with Siblings and with Friends: Links between Relationship Quality and Social Understanding', *British Journal of Developmental Psychology*, 24(1): 73–87.

Darwin, C. (1877) 'A Biographical Sketch of an Infant', *Mind, A Quarterly Review of Psychology and Philosophy*, 2(7): 285–294.

Dunn, J. (1993) *Young Children's Close Relationships: Beyond Attachment*. London: Sage.

Dunn, J. (2004) *Children's Friendships: The Beginnings of Intimacy*. Oxford: Blackwell.

Edwards, R., Gillies, V. and Horsley, N. (2014) 'Policy Briefing: The Biologisation of Poverty – Policy and Practice in Early Years Intervention', *Discover Society*, Social Research Publications.

Elias, N. (2009) 'On Human Beings and Their Emotions: A Process-Sociological Essay', in *Essays III: On Sociology and the Humanities*. Dublin: UCD Press [Collected Works, vol. 16], pp. 141–158.

Elias, N. (2010) *The Society of Individuals*. Dublin: UCD Press [Collected Works, vol. 10].

Evanson, R. T. and Maunsell, H. (1842) *A Practical Treatise on the Management and Diseases of Children*, 4th edition. Dublin: Fannin and Co.

Faircloth, C. (2011) '"It Feels Right in My Heart": Affective Accountability in Narratives of Attachment', *The Sociological Review*, 59(2): 283–302.

Field, F. (2010) *The Foundation Years: Preventing Poor Children Becoming Poor Adults. The Report of the Independent Review on Poverty and Life Chances*. London: Cabinet Office.

Fitzgerald, D., Rose, N. and Singh, I. (2014) 'Urban Health and Mental Health: Revisiting Politics, Society and Biology', *Discover Society*, Issue 5. Available at: http://discoversociety.org/2014/02/15/urban-life-and-mental-health-re-visiting-politics-society-and-biology/

Fogel, A., Garvey, A., Hsu, H.C. and West-Stroming, D. (2006) *Change Processes in Relationships: A Relational-Historical Research Approach*. Cambridge: Cambridge University Press.

Fogel, A., Hsu, H.C., Shapiro, A.F., Nelson-Goens, G.C. and Secrist, C. (2006) 'Effects of Normal and Perturbed Social Play on the Duration and Amplitude of Different Types of Infant Smiles', *Developmental Psychology*, 42(3): 459–473.

Foucault, M. (2007) *Security, Territory, Population*. New York: Picador.

Gregory, E. (2001) 'Sisters and Brothers as Language and Literacy Teachers: Synergy between Siblings Playing and Working Together', *Journal of Early Childhood Literacy*, 1(3): 301–322.

Grossmann, K., Grossmann, K.E., Fremmer-Bombik, E., Kindler, H., Scheuerer-Englisch, H. and Zimmermann, P. (2002) 'The Uniqueness of the Child–Father Attachment Relationship: Father's Sensitive and

Challenging Play as a Pivotal Variable in a 16-year Longitudinal Study', *Social Development* 11(3): 307–331.

Hall, G. S. (1883) 'Content of Childen's Minds', *Princeton Review* 2: 249–272.

Harlow, H.F., Harlow, M.K. and Hansen, E.W. (1963) 'The Maternal Affectional System of Rhesus Monkeys', in H.R. Rheingold (ed.), *Maternal Behaviour in Mammals*. New York: Wiley, pp. 254–281.

Holmes, J. (1993) *John Bowlby and Attachment Theory*. London: Routledge.

Howes, C. (1999) 'Attachment Relationships in the Context of Multiple Carers', in J. Cassidy and P.R. Shaver (eds), *Handbook of Attachment*. New York: The Guilford Press, pp. 671–687.

Howes, C. (2011) 'A Model for Studying Socialisation in Early Childhood Education and Care', in M. Kernan and E. Singer (eds), *Peer Relationships in Early Childhood Education and Care*. London: Routledge, pp. 15–26.

Hultqvist, K. and Dahlberg, G. (2001) 'Governing the Child in the New Millennium', in K. Hultqvist and G. Dahlberg (eds), *Governing the Child in the New Millennium*. London: Routledge, pp. 1–14.

Jablonka, E. and Lamb, M. (2006) *Evolution in Four Dimensions: Genetic, Epigenetic, Behavioral, and Symbolic Variation in the History of Life*. Cambridge, MA: MIT Press.

Jackson, S. and Rees, A. (2007) 'The Appalling Appeal of Nature: The Popular Influence of Evolutionary Psychology as a Problem for Sociology', *Sociology*, 41(5): 917–930.

James, A.L. (2010) 'Competition or Integration? The Next Step in Childhood Studies?', *Childhood*, 17(4): 485–499.

James, A., Jenks, C. and Prout, A. (1998) *Theorising Childhood*. Cambridge: Polity.

Jenks, C. (1996) *Childhood*. London: Routledge.

Kukla, R. (2005) *Mass Hysteria, Medicine, Culture and Women's Bodies*. New York: Roman and Littlefield.

Langston, A. (2006) 'Why Parents Matter', in L. Abbott and A. Langston (eds), *Parents Matter: Supporting the Birth to Three Framework*. Maidenhead: Open University Press, pp. 1–12.

Lee, E. (2007) 'Health, Morality, and Infant Feeding: British Mothers' Experiences of Formula Milk Use in the Early Weeks', *Sociology of Health and Illness*, 29(7): 1075–1090.

Lee, N. (2001) *Childhood and Society*. Buckingham: Open University Press.

LeVine, R.A. and Norman, K. (2008) 'Attachment in an Anthropological Perspective', in R.A. LeVine and R.S. New (eds), *Anthropology and Child Development: A Cross-Cultural Reader*. Oxford: Blackwell, pp. 127–142.

Lewis, M. (2005) 'The Child and its Family: The Social Network Model', *Human Development*, 48(1–2): 8–27.

Lewontin, R.L. (2001) 'Gene, Organism and Environment', in S. Oyama, P.E. Griffiths and R.D. Gray (eds), *Cycles of Contingency*. Cambridge, MA: MIT Press, pp. 59–66.

Lorenz, K.Z. (1957 [1935]) 'Companionship in Bird Life – Fellow Members of the Species as Releasers of Social Behaviour', in C.H. Schiller (ed.), *Instinctive Behaviour*. New York: International Universities Press, pp. 83–128.

Macmurray, J. (2012) 'Learning to be Human', *Oxford Review of Education*, 38(6): 661–674.

McConnell, M. and Moss, E. (2011) 'Attachment Across the Life Span: Factors that Contribute to Stability and Change', *Australian Journal of Educational & Developmental Psychology*, 11: 60–77.

Meloni, M. (2014) 'Biology without Biologism: Social Theory in a Postgenomic Age', *Sociology*, 48(4): 731–746.

Morss, J.B. (1990) *The Biologising of Childhood: Developmental Psychology and the Darwinian Myth*. Hove: Lawrence Erlbaum.

Moss, P. and Petrie, P. (2002) *From Children's Services to Children's Spaces: Public Policy, Children and Childhood*. London: Routledge.

Müller, G.B. (2007) 'Evo-Devo: Extending the Evolutionary Synthesis', *Nature Reviews: Genetics*, 8: 943–949.

Murphy, E. (1999) 'Breast is Best: Infant Feeding Decisions and Maternal Deviance', *Sociology of Health and Illness*, 21(2): 187–208.

Newland, L.A. and Coyl, D.D. (2010) 'Fathers' Role as Attachment Figures: An Interview with Sir Richard Bowlby', *Early Child Development and Care*, 180(1-2): 25–32.

NICHD (National Institute of Child Health and Human Development) Early Childcare Research Network (2004) 'Fathers' and Mothers' Parenting Behaviour and Beliefs as Predictors of Child Social Adjustment in the Transition to School', *Journal of Family Psychology*, 18(4): 628–638.

Oates, J., Lewis, C. and Lamb, M.E. (2005) 'Parenting and Attachment', in S. Ding and K. Littleton (eds), *Children's Personal and Social Development*. Oxford: Blackwell, pp. 11–51.

Oyama, S., Griffiths, P.E. and Gray, R.D. (2001) *Cycles of Contingency: Developmental Systems and Evolution*. Cambridge, MA: MIT Press.

Papatheodorou, T. (2009) 'Exploring Relational Pedagogy', in *Learning Together in the Early Years: Exploring Relational Pedagogy*. London: Routledge, pp. 3-18.

Parker-Rees, R. (2014) 'Playfulness and the Co-construction of Identity in the First Years', in E. Brooker, M. Blaise and S. Edwards (eds), *Sage Handbook of Play and Learning in Early Childhood*. London: Sage, pp. 366–377.

Piaget, J. (1927) *The Child's Conception of the World*. London: Routledge and Kegan Paul.

Preyer, W.T. (1882) *Die Seele des Kindes: Beobachtungen über die geistige Entwicklung des Menschen in den ersten Lebensjahren*. Leipzig: Grieben.

Prout, A. (2005) *The Future of Childhood*. London: RoutledgeFalmer.

Quilley, S. (2010) 'Integrative Levels and "The Great Evolution": Organicist Biology and the Sociology of Norbert Elias', *Journal of Classical Sociology*, 10(4): 391–419.

Reddy, V. (2008) *How Infants Know Minds*. Cambridge, MA: Harvard University Press.

Reddy, V. (2011) 'A Gaze at Grips with Me', in A. Seeman (ed.), *Joint Attention: New Developments in Psychology, Philosophy of Mind and Social Neuroscience*. Cambridge, MA: The MIT Press, pp. 137–157.

Rogoff, B. (2003) *The Cultural Nature of Human Development*. Oxford: Oxford University Press.

Rogoff, B., Paradise, R., Mejia Arauz, R., Correa-Chávez, M. and Angelillo, C. (2003) 'Firsthand Learning through Intent Participation', *Annual Review of Psychology*, 54: 175–203.

Rose, S. (1997) *Lifelines: Biology, Freedom, Determinism*. London: Penguin.

Rossetti-Ferreira, M.C., de Moraes, Z., de Oliveira, R., Campos-De-Carvalho, M.I. and Amorim, K.S. (2011) 'Peer Relations in Brazilian Daycare Centres: A New Focus for Early Childhood Education', in M. Kernan and E. Singer (eds), *Peer Relationships in Early Childhood Education and Care*. London: Routledge, pp. 74–87.

Rutter, M. (2002) 'Nature, Nurture, and Development: From Evangelism through Science toward Policy and Practice', *Child Development*, 73(1): 1–21.

Schaffer, H.R. (2004) *Introducing Child Psychology*. Oxford: Blackwell.

Schilbach, L., Timmermans, B., Reddy, V., Costall, A., Bente, G., Schlicht, T. and Vogeley, K. (2013) 'Toward a Second-person Neuroscience', *Behavioural and Brain Sciences*, 36(4): 393–462.

Stainton Rogers, R. and Stainton Rogers, W. (1992) *Stories of Childhood: Shifting Agendas of Child Concern*. New York and London: Harvester Wheatsheaf.

Starr, L. (1894) *An American Textbook on the Diseases of Children*. Philadelphia: W.B. Saunders.

Super, C.M. and Harkness, S. (1982) 'The Infant's Niche in Rural Kenya and Metropolitan America', in L.L. Adler (ed.), *Cross-Cultural Research at Issue*. New York: Academic Press, pp. 47–55.

Taylor, A. (2011) 'Reconceptualizing the "Nature" of Childhood', *Childhood*, 18(4): 420–433.

Tizard, B. (2009) 'Looking Back: The Making and Breaking of Attachment Theory', *The Psychologist*, 22(10): 902–903.

Trevarthen, C. (2005) 'Stepping Away from the Mirror: Pride and Shame in Adventures of Companionship', in C.S. Carter, L. Ahnert, K.E. Grossman, S.B. Hrdy, S.W. Porges and N. Sachser (eds), *Attachment and Bonding: A New Synthesis*. Cambridge, MA: The MIT Press, pp. 55–84.

Trevarthen, C. (2011) 'The Generation of Human Meaning', in A. Seeman (ed.), *Joint Attention: New Developments in Psychology, Philosophy of Mind and Social Neuroscience*. Cambridge: The MIT Press, pp. 73–113.

Turmel, A. (2008) *A Historical Sociology of Childhood: Developmental Thinking, Categorization and Graphic Visualization*. Cambridge: Cambridge University Press.

Valsiner, J. (2000) *Culture and Human Development*. London: Sage.

Walker, S.P., Wachs, T.D., Grantham-McGregor, S., Black, M.M., Nelson, C.A., Huffman, S.L. et al. (2011) 'Inequality in Early Childhood: Risk and Protective Factors for Early Child Development', *The Lancet*, 378: 1325–1338.

Winnicott, D.W. (1964) *The Child, the Family and the Outside World*. Harmondsworth: Penguin Books.

Winterson, J. (2011) *Why Be Happy When You Could Be Normal?* London: Jonathan Cape.

Wood, J.C. (2007) 'The Limits of Culture: Society, Evolutionary Psychology and the History of Violence', *Cultural and Social History*, 4(1): 95–114.

Woodhead, M. (2003) 'The Child in Development', in M. Woodhead and H. Montgomery (eds), *Understanding Childhood: An Interdisciplinary Approach.* Chichester: Wiley/Open University Press, pp. 85–134.

Woodhead, M. (2008) 'Childhood Studies: Past, Present and Future', in M.J. Kehilly (ed.), *An Introduction to Childhood Studies*, 2nd edition. Maidenhead: Open University Press/McGraw Hill, pp. 17–31.

World Health Organization (2003) *Global Strategy on Infant and Young Child Feeding.* Geneva: WHO.

4

GROWING UP BESIDE YOU – SOCIAL HABITUS IN EARLY CHILDHOOD

Introduction

In the last chapter I argued that sociologists of childhood need to move beyond their narrow interpretation of developmental psychology, mainly based around their critique of Piaget's age and stage approach to young children. They rejected the biological assumptions and deterministic discourse associated with this particular version of developmental psychology, arguing that we need to emphasise children's agency and social competence. Although young children can negotiate and make choices in their relationships with adults, sociologists have a tendency to underestimate that such competence is relational, learnt largely from adults and historically variable. They therefore tend to overemphasise the extent to which young children are free to determine their own actions. Moreover, such an approach tends to overlook other important developmental theories – most notably those inspired by Lev Vygotsky, the Russian developmental psychologist. Vygotsky's socio-cultural perspective emphasises mutuality in the individual–society relationship and incorporates the social environment as part of a relational system in which young children develop.

This chapter will begin by comparing the theoretical perspectives of Vygotsky and Elias, arguing that both these perspectives enrich one another in elaborating a relational perspective of young children's development in societies. Both provide a sophisticated, developmental perspective that can follow the interweaving of biological and social processes as young children learn from their parents or carers how to survive and grow in their societies. These processes are discussed in highly nuanced relational concepts that are crucial for understanding the ways in which young children grow up to become members in their different societies. We will focus on some of the key concepts that they introduced to understand the early development of language by young children.

However, Connolly (2004) argues that there remains a sense in which the notion of the 'social' in Vygotsky's work has remained largely undeveloped, ignoring broader social processes within which young children are located. He suggests that it is important to further develop Vygotsky's approach with some of the theoretical insights provided by the relational sociologist Pierre Bourdieu. Bourdieu's work is important because it provides a set of relational conceptual tools – capital, habitus and field – to investigate the shifting fields of power that affect the lives of young children, emphasising the interdependent relationships between young children, their peers and adults in changing institutional arrangements. These three core concepts are an important part of Bourdieu's attempt to overcome the traditional micro-macro divisions in sociology – they encourage us to locate and understand young children's relationships within the context of broader social structures rather than just the immediate interpersonal relationships that a young child is involved in.

We then discuss the family as the 'primary habitus' or institution where young children initially internalise ways of thinking and types of dispositions from their parents or carers. Although families are still important in the shaping of young children's lives, I will argue that in contemporary society we need to explain the extent to which young children can develop their own stocks of social capital and distinctive rules of capital conversion. With more young children spending their days in nurseries, kindergartens and day centres, there are increasing expectations about what should be considered appropriate behaviour. Studies that have looked at the daily practices of young children in day care groups and nurseries have suggested that becoming an 'acceptable' child demands a fine-tuned sensitivity to others in deeply embedded institutional contexts (Gilliam and Gulløv, 2014; Vuorisalo et al., 2015).

Quest for Synthesis

What can two very different biographical and intellectual careers have in common?

Elias was a sociologist who productively worked and lived in various European countries until the age of 93; Vygotsky was a Russian developmental psychologist influenced by the Marxist ideas of the Soviet Revolution, dying at the young age of 37 from tuberculosis. First, what is significant is that both were not only attempting a broad intellectual synthesis from within their own subject areas, but also trying to integrate disciplines that were usually considered separate and unrelated: biology, social anthropology, history and psychoanalysis, to name just a few. They argued that previous approaches in psychology or sociology had reduced social relationships to the investigation of isolated concepts, with little consideration of how factors relate to one another. For example, in studies of language development, academic specialists have separated connected processes into independent areas of study; as a result of the application of this form of analysis to verbal thinking, meaning had been divorced from sound.

To reflect complex psychological processes as activities, what was required was a significant reorientation of thought, one that would restore the dynamic and interrelated aspects of socio-psychological systems, capturing 'the movement from thought to word and from word to thought' (Vygotsky, 1987: 250). In a very similar way, Elias (2011) emphasised that traditional academic specialists like philosophers have constructed theories of knowledge and language into separate human activities, three different worlds known as language, reason and knowledge. To overcome the reduction of processes to static entities, Elias argued that these three different realms should be viewed as symbols whose function is to connect relationships between thinking, speaking and knowing.

Second, another key similarity between Elias and Vygotsky was their integration of a highly sophisticated developmental perspective. Their developmental approach not only attempted to understand the group moulding of individual children in existing societies, but also wished to explain this moulding within a wider framework that included the different stages of human development in history. Both emphasised that development is not linear, a straight path of quantitative accumulations, but a dynamic and uneven process that can give rise to new structures or qualitative changes at higher levels of organisation. In the 1920s Vygotsky and his colleagues, Alexander Luria and Alexei Leontiev, proposed a human science of psychology to stand alongside the natural sciences. The central thesis of the Russian cultural-historical school was that the structure and development of human psychological processes emerge through culturally mediated, historically developing, practical activity:

> Both planes of development – the natural and the cultural – coincide and mingle with one another. The two lines of change interpenetrate one another and form what is essentially a single line of socio-biological formation of the child's personality. To the extent that development occurs in the cultural medium, it becomes transformed into a historically conditioned biological process. (Vygotsky, 1930: 47)

'Natural' and 'Cultural' Lines of Development

Building on my argument in the previous chapter that the role of biology needs to be taken up by a relational approach which is capable of investigating the various aspects of young children's development, Cole (1998) has argued that culture should be viewed as the species-specific medium of *Homo sapiens*. Human biology and human culture should not be juxtaposed with one another – the human brain and body co-evolved over a long period of time with the complex cultural environment of the species. Cole (1996) summarises the 'either/or' aspects of these scholarly debates by asking whether language is acquired through a process of culturally mediated learning, or is a specialised domain that needs to be spurred into action. Cole argues that both the natural and the cultural lines of development need to be present for language acquisition: not only are young children born with the 'seeds' of language, they also have to participate in jointly organised activities that enable them to gain control over their environment. According to Resnick (1994: 479), the biological roots of development predominate in infancy and early childhood, while the socio-cultural roots take 'increasing control … as each individual's personal history of situations grows and initial biologically prepared structures are successfully modified'.

Moreover, this cultural context should not be seen as something outside the process of development 'as that which surrounds' but an intrinsic part of 'that which weaves together' (Cole, 1996: 132–135). Patterns of nurturance and communication do not merely influence young children's development, but are an intrinsic part of the developmental process. In Vygotsky and Luria's (1994) view, a developmental approach should be the main method used to analyse three lines of human behaviour – evolutionary, historical and ontogenetic. In each of these lines or genetic domains, different principles operate to produce a change in the type of development itself. Each stage in the formation of higher psychological processes is distinguished by a particular organisation of psychological activity. For example, when speech begins to serve as a psychological instrument for the regulation of behaviour, young children learn to use language that will enable them to plan future actions. From accompanying young children's actions in chaotic problem-solving, speech now acts as a guide to determine their future behaviour (Vygotsky, 1978).

Significantly, Vygotsky argued that the higher processes such as language cannot be reduced to inferior ones: according to Van der Veer and Valsiner (1991), Vygotsky's consistently anti-reductionist perspective can be seen as a major contribution to psychology.

Vygotsky argued that human psychological functions are organised hierarchically, with each level needing to be studied in its specifics. The biological newborn grows up in an environment composed of cultural artefacts – as a result, two 'lines' of development, the natural and the cultural, merge into a unique form of human development. Within this framework, Vygotsky (1978: 46) outlined the interweaving of two qualitatively different lines of development: 'the elementary processes, which are of biological origin, on the one hand, and the higher psychological functions, of socio-cultural origin, on the other'.

Elias and Vygotsky were also both engaged with explaining the biological framework that is necessary for young children to learn a language. I will now examine some of the concepts that they introduced to understand the development of young children as they move from communicating sound patterns to learning and eventually mastering a language. It will be argued that both these perspectives enrich one another in developing a relational perspective of young children's development in societies.

Learning to Speak a Language

Young children must learn a language in order to survive. The capacity of young human beings to steer their conduct by means of learned knowledge gave them a great evolutionary advantage over other species who were unable to accomplish this at all or only to a very limited extent. Elias (2011) refers to this process as humankind's 'symbol emancipation'. A young child develops into a human being and is integrated into a particular society by learning to produce words and sentences which are understood by others:

> They [children] learn to regulate their own speech behaviour and, indeed, their own behaviour generally in accordance with the common code of producing and retrieving articulated sound-patterns as messages for and from other people which prevail in their society. This is the crucial aspect of the interlocking of nature and society in the structure of human languages. (Elias, 2011: 71)

How do these 'sound patterns' in young children gradually become overlaid as a means of communication? According to Vygotsky (1987), a pre-intellectual stage in the development of young children's speech can be primarily characterised by an emotional form of behaviour, one that is displayed through crying and babbling. During this stage, laughing, pointing and gesture emerge as a complex form of infant interaction with adults: when an infant cries or reaches for an object, adults attribute meaning to that behaviour. Within this context, Vygotsky (1981) discussed the emergence of indicative gestures – in the confusion that surrounds infants in the first few months of their lives, parents point and carry their children to objects and places of adaptive significance. He illustrated this conceptual idea through the development of the pointing gesture in infants, arguing that this gesture develops when a mother misreads her infant's unsuccessful grasping for a remote object as the infant's command to the mother to give her the object. This experience is repeated again and again. When the infant notices the link between the mother extending her hand and bringing a desired object she begins to instrumentally extend her hand for getting remote objects. These acts function to communicate their needs to caretakers – very young children are involved in social activity even before they have the capacity to use or respond adequately to communicative devices.

Symbolic and Meaningful Speech

Once young children have moved from vocalised reflexes and imitating sounds, the symbolic function of speech occurs: they discover the functional use of words as a means of naming objects for expressing certain wishes and gaining control of their environment (Vygotsky, 1987; Vygotsky and Luria, 1994). In young children's development, a stage of language acquisition is marked by a rapid accumulation of words, which children repeat and invent when they meet situations where previously heard words do not fit. Like Elias, Vygotsky argued that a crucial aspect of this developmental change was the manner in which previously separate and elementary biological functions are integrated into new functional learning systems. For young children to make any advancement in intellectual behaviour they must go beyond learned reactions that fail to overcome some difficulty or barrier.

Vygotsky (1987) argued that relatively early in speech development two planes of development move towards one another to merge: young children become increasingly aware that the living process of meaningful speech is composed of auditory and semantic aspects. At the auditory level, they master vocal speech by progressing from single words to two word phrases and then to simple sentences. During this early stage, the word is an 'oral indicative gesture', its function to designate or isolate one aspect of a situation from others. Like indicative gestures, words have no meaning outside the concrete contexts in which they are used. At the semiotic level, meanings which are inherent in young children's utterances begin as full sentences and only gradually become differentiated to express phrases or single words. This process of 'meaning-making' is a crucial stage in adapting to society – young children learn to use pre-determined tools of language to become more communicative and engage fully in societal behaviour.

In mastering cultural knowledge, young children can take a step towards emancipation from nature: whereas animals are almost fully dependent on the inheritance of genetically based traits, humans can adapt and learn new skills. However, young children not only acquire tools that have been transmitted from one generation to another, but create new ones – what Knox (1994) refers to as a 'Second Symbol System', words or signs that substitute for objects. This system is first used by human beings to communicate with or control each other and then internalised to regulate their own behaviour in new situations. A good example of the way that symbols help to orientate human behaviour is the concept 'moon' which refers to a constantly changing form in the sky. Elias asks how our ancestors could achieve an integrating concept that would synthesise the different shapes in the sky? His answer is that, 'It could only have resulted from a long process of learning, of the growth of people's stock of experiences, some of which recurred again and again and, over the generations, were remembered as recurring' (Elias, 2007: 55).

Self-regulation and Internalisation

As mentioned in Chapter 2 Elias (2006) made an important conceptual distinction between the term 'evolution', which should refer to biological processes that are genetic and relatively fixed, and 'development', social processes that are more malleable and subject to change. In his attempt to identify some of the distinguishing characteristics of human beings that 'animal psychologists' (ethologists) have ignored, Elias mentions a unique human capacity 'for controlling and modifying drives and affects in a great variety of ways as part of a learning process' (Elias, 2007: 125). This capacity for developing forms of self-restraint is central to Elias' argument in *On the Process of Civilisation* (2012): the increasing social constraint towards self-constraint is related to more demanding standards of self-control. Social pressures lead to more self-control, with the behaviour of individual people being regulated 'in an increasingly differentiated, more even and more stable manner' (Elias, 2012: 406).

An integral aspect of this civilising process is that young children should eventually grow up through their own self-regulation. Here is where we can directly compare the long-term movement from 'external control' to 'self-control' with Vygotsky's explanation of the central role of internalisation processes in the acquisition of language. In order for young children to regulate their own speech behaviour and understand the same symbols as adults, speech is internalised, becoming a vital part of the higher psychological processes – it organises, unifies and integrates disparate aspects of young children's behaviour, such as perception, problem-solving and memory:

> The greatest change in children's capacity to use language as a problem-solving tool takes place somewhat later in their development, when socialised speech is *turned inward*. Instead of appealing to the adult, children appeal to themselves; language thus takes on an *intrapersonal function* in addition to its *interpersonal use*. (Vygotsky, 1978: 26, emphases in original)

How are these processes 'turned inward', enabling young children to develop their use of language? In this context, Vygotsky (1987) explained the important process of internalisation for understanding the cultural evolution of young children's thinking. What makes thinking possible is 'inner speech', a distinctive form of verbal thinking that mediates between word and thought. Two important processes are interwoven in inner speech: the transition from external communication to inner dialogue and the translation of intimate thoughts into a linguistic and communicative form. This concept of inner speech is a type of speech that is 'mute' and 'silent', involving no vocalisation. In inner speech, word sense – which is dependent on the context of speech – develops and becomes predominant over meaning.

Elias (2011) uses similar imagery to discuss internalisation in *The Symbol Theory*. In language communication, one of the functions of the term 'thinking' is to refer to the capacity of human beings to put through their paces symbols anticipating a sequence of possible future actions without their performance in reality. At this level, thought is not easily recognisable as a flow of voicelessly produced sound–symbols, an abbreviated version of the audible use of language that can be converted at any time into spoken language. These forms of abbreviated thinking are associated with the manipulation of stored memory images: according to Elias, these do not have to be set out step by step, but can be telescoped, recalled and used when the occasion demands.

Although there are important similarities in Elias's and Vygotsky's accounts of internalisation, a distinctive emphasis can be identified. It is important to note that whereas Elias (2011: 99) discussed the conversion of spoken language into the voiceless language of thought as a 'most easily' convertible process, Vygotsky (1987: 267) viewed this process as much more gradual, emerging from the development of egocentric speech in young children. There is 'no simple transition toward a telegraphic style', but a tendency towards a form of abbreviation where the predicate and related words are preserved. This distinction may be due to the fact that Elias is discussing a longer-term process that has already been mastered by adults, while Vygotsky, basing his results on experiments with young children, is uncovering some of the complex layers that they have to learn before achieving similar capabilities.

Social Habitus in Early Childhood

So far we have discussed some of the innovative concepts that Elias and Vygotsky used to explain a universal process of humankind, the early development of language. However, Connolly (2004) has argued that there has been a tendency in Vygotskian research not to deal adequately with the complexity of social relations within which young children are located. Such work remains embedded in psychological ways of thinking and therefore has a rather limited understanding of the social. He identifies three major problems with this overall Vygotskian framework that need to be addressed. First, there is an emphasis on individual agency underpinning these accounts: we need to understand how young children's thoughts and behaviour are influenced and shaped by the broader social and cultural contexts around them. Second, there is a tendency to depict the social simply in terms of interpersonal relations – we should develop sociological concepts that can help understand the role that institutions play in influencing what young children learn. Third, culture itself is taken for granted and provides little space for an analysis of power relations and the way that this influences what young children learn and how they develop.

Connolly (2004) suggests that we need to turn to Bourdieu's sociological perspective in order to include the social habitus within which young children are located. The social habitus can be understood as a set of predispositions to ways of thinking and behaving that have been acquired over time through experience. According to Bourdieu (1990), we can best understand social development and change as taking place through the ongoing struggles that exist over a range of scarce goods and resources, which are not simply economic but also take on social and cultural forms. He conceived of four different types of capital which are often deeply interrelated and partly transposable: economic capital, 'which is immediately and directly convertible into money and may be institutionalised in the form of property rights' (Bourdieu, 1986: 243); cultural capital, which consists primarily of what is to be perceived as legitimate knowledge and behaviour and may be institutionalised in the form of educational qualifications; social capital, which relates to the prestige and influence gained through relationships and connections with powerful others; and symbolic capital, which represents the status and honour that is associated with the acquisition of one or more forms of capital once they have been perceived and recognised as legitimate by others.

Central to the concept of capital is its exchange value and its capacity through investment of time and effort to be converted from economic capital into both social and cultural capital. This was outlined in Bourdieu and Passeron's (1977) early work on education, where, for example, economic capital enables parents to send their young children to private schools to learn and appropriate certain valued forms of cultural capital. The acquisition of both economic and cultural capital enables a young child to develop valued relationships with powerful people and acquire certain positions within society. Cultural capital has particular currency in the field of education, comprising embodied (dispositions, sets of meaning and modes of thinking), objectified (access to cultural goods such as art and literature) and institutionalised forms (educational or academic qualifications), which are given recognition by those already dominant within a particular field. Those with the 'recognised' cultural capital are deemed competent in their knowledge and confident in their capacity to generate long-term benefits from their investment in education.

In an important article, Serre and Wagner (2015) offer an approach to cultural capital that emphasises its relational dimension. They argue that there is more at stake in Pierre Bourdieu's differentiation between kinds of capital than merely conceiving of social space as multi-dimensional by taking the variety of available resources behind their accumulation into account. The concept of cultural capital is mainly intended to make us think about mechanisms for legitimation. Contrary to what the most common uses of the notion of capital might lead us to think, capital is not a simple quantity of symbolic or material goods, defined once and for all, leaving only its unequal distribution to be measured: it is mainly a social relationship of domination that has important consequences within a specific field.

Serre and Wagner (2015) therefore claim that sites of cultural pro-duction (especially schools) have the function of legitimating power and keeping social order. The cultural capital that Bourdieu identified is less defined by its content (legitimate practices, educational qualifications) than by how it is acquired, which naturalises domination and makes it invisible. This is why it is so important to explain all the different aspects of cultural capital – incorporation, institutionalisation, objectification – as they relate to distinct and complementary mechanisms of domination. Incorporation presupposes a long period of invisible inculcation work from the youngest age, characteristic of incorporated cultural capital as it appears in language, knowledge and habits. Institutionalisation is tied to the power of guarantee vested in institutions of learning. Objectification, by the ownership of cultural goods, manifests capital's patrimonial dimen-sion. These mechanisms guarantee cultural capital's effectiveness when it is 'used as a weapon and as a stake in struggles' (Bourdieu, 1979: 5).

However this process of institutionalised education, as Bourdieu has argued, only represents one of the ways in which the distribution of power across social groups is achieved. Alongside the school, young children will come to learn and internalise a particular way of thinking and behaving through their family relationships as well as through the broader experiences gained through the wider community. Connolly and Healy's (2004) ethnographic case study of two groups of 7–8-year-old working-class girls living in Belfast, Northern Ireland showed that the school itself played only a partial role in influencing their educa-tional and career aspirations. Of equal significance was the influence of the local neighbourhoods within which the young girls lived. Their emerging gendered habitus was constructed through discourses on romance, marriage, motherhood and childhood rather than a concern with their education and future careers. To explain this influence, they used Bourdieu's (1990) concept of symbolic violence. Symbolic violence is a process whereby individuals can contribute towards their own sub-ordination by gradually accepting and internalising those very ideas and structures that tend to subordinate them.

'Primary' and 'Secondary' Habitus

Wacquant (2014) has brought another important nuance to this concept of habitus by drawing our attention to Bourdieu's (2000: 161) later emphasis on its malleability, 'Habitus change constantly as a function of new experiences'. A key aspect of the concept of habitus is that it incorporates past experiences which are modified by present ones, as well as a sense of a probable future (Bourdieu, 1990), although early influences always bear more weight.

Relations between socialisation and social position remain central in more pliable notions of habitus, emphasising both its layered nature and its restructuring as an ongoing process.

Wacquant (2014) argues that we need to elaborate on Bourdieu's distinction between primary and secondary habitus, introduced in his work on education and underlying his analysis of the nexus of class and taste in *Distinction* (1984). The primary habitus is the set of dispositions one acquires in early childhood, slowly and imperceptibly, through familial immersion; the schemes of action and perception that have been transferred during childhood are an education that is linked to the parents' social position in the social space. Therefore, the primary habitus is about 'internalising the external' as the parents' modes of thinking, feeling and behaving that are linked to their position in the social space are internalised in the child's own habitus. This is what Bourdieu (1977) also refers to as *class habitus* and reflects the different positions people have in society, leading to different lifestyles' tastes and interests among social classes (Bourdieu, 1999).

The primary habitus is also fashioned by tacit and diffuse 'pedagogical labour with no precedent'; it constitutes our social personality as well as 'the basis for the ulterior constitution of any other habitus' (Bourdieu and Passeron, 1977: 42–46). Pedagogical labour is about transformation, who defines what shape it will take and how it is experienced in practice by young children. Bourdieu captures these tensions when he speaks of social spaces as fields of struggle, caught between forces of transformation and preservation and depending on access to power and resources. By placing habitus in a field, Bourdieu provides a means of resisting the seductions of the notion of a self-created and autonomous subject, contending that biographies do not explain artistic, religious or political phenomena – the behaviour of an individual must be analysed relationally according to the field in which other agents are positioned. People act in a field that moulds them, biographical events being constituted according to placement and displacement within social spaces (Silva, 2016).

Bourdieu's relational understanding of the organisation of the social is presented through field theory, where the position of an agent in a field can only be understood in relation to other positions in that field. Practices are relational, causes are always interdependent and no investigator's preconceived assertion of hierarchical relations of causal dependency informs the relational organisation of the social (Crossley, 2011). When placing themselves and objects within a field, agents follow an ordering of relations that is structural and objective. Individuals are positioned independently of their will and intentions, even though their choices *modify* their original placement.

Wacquant (2014) argues that the primary habitus is a springboard for the subsequent acquisition of a secondary habitus, an organisational system of transposable schemata which bear the mark of much effort and self-discipline. The *secondary habitus* is built on the primary habitus and especially results from one's education at school and university, but also from other life experiences. The primary habitus as 'embodied history, internalized as second nature and so forgotten as history' (Bourdieu, 1990: 56) never loses its impact and always influences the development of the secondary habitus.

This important distinction between primary and secondary habitus is similar to the contrast made by Bourdieu (1984: 65–68) between 'the two modes of acquisition of culture', the familial and the academic, the experiential and the didactic, which indelibly stamp one's relation to cultural capital. Lizardo (2004) offers a very helpful way of explaining how these flexible schemata or schemas have specific meanings that can help to illuminate the subtlety of the concept of habitus and its important application for understanding the lives of young children. He explores the little recognised influence of Jean Piaget on Bourdieu's thinking, arguing that a great deal of the conceptual apparatus of the *habitus* can be traced back to his distinctive blend of structuralism and developmental cognitive psychology.

For Piaget, the child's cognitive development is driven by a constant process of assimilation of new information and accommodation of pre-existing structures to fit recurring but not necessarily identical situations in the material and social worlds. The concepts of assimilation and accommodation were at the heart of his relational perspective. Young children are inherently incomplete: they need nourishment in relation to the environment in order to move towards equilibration. Since no form of nourishment is itself complete, they must accept it, changing the form of nourishment whilst at the same time changing themselves. In the dynamics of this relationship, both young children and their environment change in relation to each other. Piaget's theory is therefore best understood as a relational-historical process (Fogel et al., 2006).

Piaget as a Relational Thinker

This repositioning of Piaget's perspective as a relational thinker is intended as an important counter-critique to the dominant sociological perspectives of childhood that were criticised in the previous chapter, where I discussed how sociologists of childhood had traditionally rejected most forms of 'developmentalism', especially those based on the Piagetian perspective, as a 'stage' and 'age' approach to young children's development. The contemporary popularisation of Piaget as a developmental psychologist who proposed a static stage theory of infant cognitive development is an impoverished image (Kitchener, 1991), which does not take into consideration his attempted syntheses of physics, biology, psychology and epistemology in *Biology and Knowledge* (1971) and his philosophy of science in *Psychogenesis and the History of Science* (Piaget and Garcia, 1989). He was a polymath whose writings defied disciplinary lines and who left an indelible mark on both the Anglo-Saxon and continental scientific fields.

If we re-focus our attention on Piaget's (1970) concept of a *psychological structure* we can usefully apply the relational concepts of field and internalised dispositions in *habitus* as an important theoretical framework for developing a sociology of early childhood. For Piaget (1954) schemes are conceptualised as patterns of action or thought that emerge out of the relationship between young children and their environment. As patterns of action within the environment, schemes are relational procedures – they are the way that young children engage with and come to know their environment. His explanation of change was disequilibration – the young child perceives that something is missing or incomplete in the relationship and orients his or her activity to something that is more likely to realise their intention. For example, when a baby notices that her kicks on the side of a crib make the mobile move she continues to kick with the newly found intention of moving the mobile.

Piaget's main emphasis was not on cognitive structures as static representations, but on the generation of *bodily schemas* and *operations*, through which the young child is then able to transform those representational structures into plans of action in the world, acquiring new cognitive structures from the feedback obtained from her practical action. In the long run, as schemes become more articulated and differentiated in relation to the environment, they become at the same time more linked and integrated with other schemes. Piaget considered knowledge to be primarily an *operative process*, with cognitive development being influenced by the interplay of different structural systems, some bodily-motor and some symbolic. He argued that cognitive development tends towards an *equilibrium* or balance between accommodation and assimilation processes.

As a consequence, the young child becomes more linked with his or her environment through an increasing set of relational schemes.

Lizardo (2004) argues that Piaget's major influence on Bourdieu's conception of *habitus* is his emphasis that knowledge and 'higher' levels of symbolic thought arise from these bodily schemas and practices which consist primarily of *internalised structures* that correspond with reality. He suggests that we can identify two principal themes in Bourdieu's thinking about *habitus* and the origins of practical action: first, belief, both in the sense of subjective harmony and objective coordination between the internal and the external, is a bodily phenomenon; and second, practical action arises out of the operation of motor and operational schemes. The key idea borrowed by Bourdieu from Piaget consists of the notion that the body itself can be both the site and the primary source of operations that come to acquire increasing generality and flexibility through experience, but which can also become conserved through sustained repetition. For example, a young child might begin with a simple set of behavioural responses, grasping or sucking, that after continual attunement to the environment come to be deployed in a wider class of situations and thus become a generalised bodily schema. Therefore it becomes important to explore how dispositions in early childhood are acquired in the primary habitus, a socially produced cognitive structure, composed of systems of embodied schemas that generate the actions of young children.

McCarthy and Prokhovnik (2014) have also explored the relational aspects of embodiment that encompass actively enfleshed beings, incorporating the felt and sensory qualities of experience and its everyday practices. They view Blackman and Venn's (2010: 14) idea that 'bodies should be defined by their capacities to affect and be affected' as a radical form of relationality, drawing attention to 'entanglements' of relationality which subvert ideas of relationships as 'an "interaction effect" between pre-existing entities' (Blackman and Venn, 2010: 10). This embodied relationality allows us to consider a close, enfleshed, relationship as generating an 'us' that helps to shape the 'me' and 'you', constructed through diverse cultural and personal resources. While 'you' and 'I' potentially have multiple identities, 'us' is a field of emotional intensity between 'me' and 'you', expressed in an embodied orientation which includes but is not reducible to an affective attunement.

Conversion of Capitals

We can further develop the concept of the primary habitus by exploring how young children are able to convert and use their own capitals within early years settings. While one of the strengths of Bourdieu's work is his acknowledgement of the lack of convertibility among different types of capital, he tends to overemphasise exchange value over use-value: action always brings the actor some kind of advantage (Skeggs, 2004). For Bourdieu (1986), the connections that make up social capital are only useful to individual actors if they can be effectively mobilised to serve their self-interests. Hence, social capital is never pursued for its intrinsic value but for its ability to be converted into other more highly desirable forms of capital. While Bourdieu appears to acknowledge that the family is a 'site where people refuse to calculate and the pursuit of equivalence in exchanges is suspended' (1984: 22), his conceptualisation of social capital, in terms of its exchange value, makes it difficult for him to fully consider the importance of use-values.

Skeggs (2004) suggests that we can explore use-values through emotions which as a type of capital can be defined 'as the stock of emotional resources built up over time within families and which children could draw upon' (Reay, 2004: 61). While Bourdieu rarely refers to emotional capital in his own work, he does describe practical and symbolic work which generates devotion, generosity and solidarity, arguing that 'this work falls more particularly to women, who are responsible for maintaining relationships' (Bourdieu, 1998: 68). Emotions can be regarded as resources which can be circulated, accumulated and exchanged for other forms of capital within a particular field that allows those resources to 'count'.

Reay (2004) contends that, in common with other forms of capital, there are generational aspects of emotional capital which are built up in families over time. However, unlike cultural, economic, social and symbolic capital, the concept of emotional capital disrupts neat links between increases in capital and educational success. It does not necessarily rise in parallel with increased social status and appears to be generated by very different practices according to mothers' past and current social class. This class-based variability means that some working-class mothers would appear to be better able to pass on emotional capital to their children when they achieve a degree of disengagement from the educational pressures common among middle-class mothers. In her studies, Reay (2004) noticed that intense emotional involvement in children's schooling often produced small returns for the working-class mothers relative to their middle-class counterparts because other key factors such as educational knowledge and confidence, material resources and social capital are not available. Some working-class mothers appeared to emphasise children's emotional well-being over educational achievement. High levels of emotional capital were being generated in the mother–child relationship around schooling, but levels of cultural capital remained relatively low (Reay, 2000, 2004).

Nevertheless, this still leaves unexplored how young children accumulate their own stocks of social capital through strategic use of networks. Leonard (2005) is very helpful for drawing our attention to the way that social capital may have different rules of conversion for young children compared to adults. As Qvortrup (1994: 4) points out, 'the adult world does not recognize children's praxis, because competence is defined merely in relation to adults' praxis – a suggestion which is all the more powerful since adults are in a sovereign position to define competence'. Young children may experience specific difficulties in converting social capital into other forms because conceptions of children as 'naturally incompetent' may prevent them from accumulating stocks of social capital that adults recognise as having exchange value.

Devine (2009), for example, considered how migrant children in Irish primary schools were not merely receptors of their family's capitals but active generators, contributing to processes of capital accumulation through their negotiation and positioning between home and school. Older siblings spent time doing homework with younger siblings – especially helping with Irish – and were also actively involved in caring for younger children when parents worked in the afternoons and evenings. Where parents were not fluent in English, or had difficulty accessing their own social networks, it was the young children who acted as mediators – teaching their parents English, acting as translators or introducing them to Irish parents.

Devine particularly noticed that friendships were important sources of social capital, facilitating access to networks that provided relief from the demands of formal learning, as well as support and knowledge when challenges emerge. These friendships gave young children a feeling of belonging and 'getting on' in their everyday lives in school. The 'durable obligations' (Bourdieu, 1986: 249) built up through these social networks ensured that they could draw on their friends to help them with school work, especially homework, as well as 'defend' them if they were being racially abused. It therefore seems that in young children's peer groups, especially where economic capital is not directly used, the importance of social capital is emphasised. If a young child has a recognised position in a friendship network, it is easier to obtain access to other capitals that others have already gained in related fields.

Peer Groups and Capital Accumulation

Only a few researchers have examined young children's peer groups and capital accumulation in early childhood institutions from a Bourdieusian framework (see Connolly, 2000, 2004; Palludan, 2007). Palludan (2007), for example, examines how kindergarten children are differentiated and segregated through vocal practices and processes. Her argument is that different groups of young children have unequal access to resources for generating respectability and obtaining recognition in a specific, linguistic market. Bourdieu (1995) argues that linguistic practices should always be interpreted as an encounter between linguistic habitus on the one hand, and the structures of the linguistic market, which are forms of recognition with specific sanctions and censorship, on the other. By using the term 'market', Bourdieu (1993) emphasises that it is not only important to speak correctly in the social space; if your linguistic contribution is to carry weight in a specific context, it is important that you use socially accepted expressions and master the art of speaking in a way that counts.

Palludan (2007) uses Bourdieu's concept of a 'linguistic habitus' to distinguish between two different language tones, a teaching tone and an exchange tone, that were practised in a Danish kindergarten. The teaching tone can be described as the vocal form that, from the adult's perspective, enables them to establish and maintain a language-based community even if the young child has little or no knowledge of Danish. The exchange tone is typically found in situations where the ethnic majority children (the Danes) and adults converse – both sides ask questions and give answers. One of her important findings was that adults are continually prone to adopting teaching tones with young children whose first language is not Danish, even when they are quite competent in Danish. Yet at the same time they tend to use exchange tones with young children whose first language is Danish. Despite the best attempts to include all the kindergarten children, the adults contributed to processes that reproduced a socio-cultural hierarchy amongst young children.

Vuorisalo (2011) also focuses on the production of hierarchies amongst young children when she argues that contemporary day care should be considered as a relational space in which they carve out positions for themselves in relation to their peers and adults. She analysed the primary habitus of 5–7-year-old children during their interactions in a day care centre and pre-school in a small Finnish town, where each child participates in a network of relationships, struggling for recognition in a rapidly changing field. Within these relational networks, young children utilise a range of resources, transforming them into valued capital that makes a difference to their relationships. Although the pre-school is not an autonomous field, her findings suggest that the pre-school space may have a degree of autonomy because the capitals that are valued and given legitimate 'currency' among young children are not directly reproduced from the resources of the families themselves.

A distinctive aspect of the pre-school field is that the evaluation of resources is more arbitrary among young children than adults where 'changes may be quick and values often unstable' (Vuorisalo, 2011: 43). Objective cultural capital does not always have long-lasting value for young children as recognition has to be endlessly 'affirmed and reaffirmed' through everyday social exchange. Young children have to use a great deal of energy and attention to become aware of the currency of various resources in a given field and orient themselves to maximum exchange. In a peer-group culture, where a used sweet-wrapping may gain value as a resource, active participation is a way for them to be involved in the ongoing game where the values of resources are defined. As part of a young children's habitus, recognising the game played in the field requires embodied cultural capital, dispositions and practices which guide participation in what and how to act.

Conclusions

This chapter began by focusing on how we can explain how young children learn to communicate and become part of a shared social habitus. I focused on language development, because it draws attention to how social and psychological functions are intimately connected and enable young children to actively organise their own development with the guidance and support of skilled partners. For Elias and Vygotsky, a central feature of this development is the relationship between 'verbal thinking' and spoken language or how communication becomes turned into silent or inner speech. Such internalisation processes are crucial for understanding the ways in which young children become active learners. However, I argued that Vygotsky still does not fully overcome some of the persistent dualities that remain in his explanation of the relationship between the 'individual' child and 'society', or 'internal' and 'external' aspects of social development: the individual child is still viewed as a container of self-contained higher mental functions, whose thoughts, feelings and behaviour are relatively detached from the broader institutions that influence his or her life.

Nevertheless, Vygotsky's ideas can be built upon and deepened by using some of the key theoretical concepts that Bourdieu develops in his relational sociology. One important concept in his work was his attempt, through the notion of habitus, to develop a conceptual tool that avoided the construction of dualisms regarding the individual and society or structure and agency. By tracing the historical genesis of Bourdieu's thought, we re-positioned Piaget's perspective as a relational thinker. We then usefully applied the relational concepts of field and internalised dispositions in *habitus* as an important theoretical framework for developing a sociology of early childhood. The social habitus refers here to the internalisation of wider structures and processes manifested through the routines and taken-for-granted actions of young children: the longer an individual child is located within a particular set of relationships, the more likely she or he is to develop a practical sense of how to behave and act in certain ways.

Then we turned our attention to the family as the 'primary habitus', where young children initially derive modes of thinking and types of dispositions from their parents or carers. Although families are still important institutions in the accumulation and transmission of economic, cultural, social and symbolic capital, I argued that in contemporary society young children are not mere receptors of their family's capitals, but active generators through their structural positioning in early years settings. These settings can usefully be viewed within the concept of a shifting and competitive field – one that enables us to develop an understanding of when and where particular forms of capital become eminent and valued or diminish in importance and eventually decline.

In addition to the relation between different types of capital, Bourdieu (1986) emphasises processes in which one form of capital can be transformed into another. Play, long characterised as one of the defining features of childhood, is one very distinctive field where we can observe young children utilising and transforming resources as capital. In the next chapter we will discuss the transgressive aspects of young children's play, exploring through their peer cultures the tensions that exist between their desire for independence from adults and their simultaneous dependence on them.

DISCUSSION ACTIVITY

Qualander Case Study, No Five Fingers are Alike

The Qualander are nomads who travel around from village to village in Pakistan. According to one of Berland's (1982: 111) informants 'our children first use language to abuse, then learn to talk'. Berland observed no language restrictions in their daily speech, noting that some of their expressions would be shocking compared to the politeness that is expected in a British context. For example, a sister expressing anger or affection to a brother would say, 'You have a face like a monkey.'

1. How do Qualander children learn to speak? In what way can this example be used to explain Bourdieu's concept of habitus?

2. 'Through their words and deeds young children learn from adults.' Discuss this statement with examples from your own experience of 'growing up'.

3. Why are adults so concerned with the regulation of young children's speech?

Further Reading

Daniel Everett (2008) *Don't Sleep, There are Snakes: Life and Language in the Amazonian Jungle*. London: Profile Books.

There is no easy way to categorise this amazing story of a Christian missionary's linguistic adventures in the Amazon forest. In 1977 Daniel Everett took his young family to live with the Pirahãs, a small and remote tribe in the Brazilian Amazon with one of the least understood languages in the world. Pirahã is a tonal language and many words appear to take an arbitrarily changing form. He persisted over the course of several decades and gradually mastered the language. In the process he learned that the Pirahã were not interested in the Bible, Christ or, indeed, any abstract philosophy or experience that they could not themselves witness. What determines the shape of the language, its basic architecture, is the surrounding culture.

Mari Vuorisalo, Niina Rutanen and Raija Raittila (2015) 'Constructing Relational Space', *Early Years*, 35(1): 1–13.

A good example of some recent attempts by sociologists to apply Bourdieu's theoretical perspective to early childhood. It examines early childhood education by applying relational-spatial perspectives to everyday life in educational institutions. The authors investigate the dynamic process in the construction of space and illustrate their argument by using selected ethnographic data drawn from two day care centres in Finland. Their analysis shows how young children and educators engage in the process of constructing space from diverse positions and the way that the institutional context is embedded within this process.

H. Colley (2006) 'Learning to Labour with Feeling: Class, Gender and Emotion in Childcare Education and Training', *Contemporary Issues in Early Childhood*, 7(1): 15–29.

One of the few articles that applies emotional capital to an early years context by investigating a group of childcare students throughout their two-year course. In analysing its official, unwritten and hidden curricula, Colley reveals how gender and class combine with vocational education and training to construct imperatives about the development of 'correct' emotions in childcare. She compares theorisations of emotional capital and emotional labour, arguing that we need social rather than individualised understandings of how feelings are put to work.

References

Berland, J.C. (1982) *No Five Fingers are Alike*. Cambridge, MA: Harvard University Press.

Blackman, L. and Venn, C. (2010) 'Affect', *Body & Society*, 16(1): 7–28.

Bourdieu, P. (1977) *Outline of a Theory Practice*. Cambridge: Cambridge University Press.

Bourdieu, P. (1979) 'Les trois états du capital culturel', *Actes de la recherche en sciences sociales*, 30(30): 3–6.

Bourdieu, P. (1984) *Distinction: A Social Critique of the Judgment of Taste*. Cambridge, MA: Harvard University Press.

Bourdieu, P. (1986) 'The Forms of Capital', in J.G. Richardson (ed.), *Handbook of Theory and Research for the Sociology of Education*. New York: Greenwood Press, pp. 241–258.

Bourdieu, P. (1990) *The Logic of Practice*. Cambridge: Polity Press.

Bourdieu, P. (1993) *Sociology in Question*. London: Sage.

Bourdieu, P. (1995) *Language and Symbolic Power*. Cambridge, MA: Harvard University Press.

Bourdieu, P. (1998) 'The Family Spirit', appendix of Chapter 3: 'Rethinking the State', in *Practical Reason*. Cambridge: Polity Press.

Bourdieu, P. (2000) *Pascalian Meditations*. Cambridge: Polity Press.

Bourdieu, P. and Passeron, J.C. (1977) *Reproduction in Education, Society and Culture*. London: Sage.

Cole, M. (1996) *Cultural Psychology: A Once and Future Discipline*. Cambridge, MA: Harvard University Press.

Cole, M. (1998) 'Culture in Development', in M. Woodhead, D. Faulkner and K. Littleton (eds), *Cultural Worlds of Early Childhood*. London: Routledge, pp. 11–33.

Connolly, P. (2000) 'Racism and Young Girls' Peer-group Relations: The Experiences of South Asian Girls', *Sociology*, 34(3): 499–519.

Connolly, P. (2004) *Boys and Schooling in the Early Years*. London: Routledge Falmer.

Connolly, P. and Healy, J. (2004) 'Symbolic Violence and the Neighbourhood: The Educational Aspirations of 7–8 year old Working-class Girls', *British Journal of Sociology*, 55(4): 511–529.

Crossley, N. (2011) *Towards Relational Sociology*. London: Routledge.

Devine, D. (2009) 'Mobilising Capitals? Migrant Children's Negotiation of their Everyday Lives in School', *British Journal of Sociology of Education*, 30(5): 521–535.

Elias, N. (2006) *The Court Society*. Dublin: UCD Press [Collected Works, vol. 2].

Elias, N. (2007) *An Essay on Time*. Dublin: UCD Press [Collected Works, vol. 9].

Elias, N. (2011) *The Symbol Theory*. Dublin: UCD Press [Collected Works, vol. 13].

Elias, N. (2012) *On the Process of Civilisation*. Dublin: UCD Press [Collected Works, vol. 3].

Fogel, A., Garvey, A., Hsu, H.C. and West-Stroming, D. (2006) *Change Processes in Relationships: A Relational-Historical Research Approach*. Cambridge: Cambridge University Press.

Gilliam, L. and Gulløv, E. (2014) 'Making Children "Social": Civilising Institutions in the Danish Welfare State', *Human Figurations*, 3(1). Available at: http://hdl.handle.net/2027/spo.11217607.0003.103

Kitchener, R.F. (1991) 'Jean Piaget: The Unknown Sociologist?', *The British Journal of Sociology*, 42(3): 421–442.

Knox, J.E. (1994) 'Introduction', in L.S. Vygotsky and A.R. Luria, *Studies on the History of Behaviour: Ape, Primitive, and Child*. London: Lawrence Erlbaum.

Leonard, M. (2005) 'Children, Childhood and Social Capital: Exploring the Links', *Sociology*, 39(4): 605–622.

Lizardo, O. (2004) 'The Cognitive Origins of Bourdieu's *Habitus*', *Journal for the Theory of Social Behaviour*, 34(4): 375–401.

McCarthy, J.R. and Prokhovnik, R. (2014) 'Embodied Relationality and Caring after Death', *Body and Society*, 20(2): 18–43.

Palludan, C. (2007) 'Two Tones: The Core of Inequality in Kindergarten', *International Journal of Early Childhood*, 39(1): 75–91.

Piaget, J. (1954) *The Construction of Reality in the Child*. New York: Basic Books.

Piaget, J. (1970) *Structuralism*. New York: Basic Books.

Piaget, J. (1971) *Biology and Knowledge: An Essay on the Relations between Organic Regulations and Cognitive Processes*. Chicago: University of Chicago Press.

Piaget, J. and Garcia, R. (1989) *Psychogenesis and the History of Science*. New York: Columbia University Press.

Qvortrup, J. (1994) 'Childhood Matters: An Introduction', in J. Qvortrup, M. Bardy, G. Sgritta and H. Wintersberger (eds), *Childhood Matters: Social Theory, Practice and Politics*. Aldershot: Avebury, pp. 1–24.

Reay, D. (2000) 'A Useful Extension of Bourdieu's Conceptual Framework? Emotional Capital as a Way of Understanding Mothers' Involvement in their Children's Education', *The Sociological Review*, 48(4): 568–585.

Reay, D. (2004) 'Gendering Bourdieu's Concepts of Capitals? Emotional Capital, Women and Social Class', *Sociological Review*, 52 (Issue Supplement): 57–74.

Resnick, L.B. (1994) 'Situated Rationalism: Biological and Social Preparation for Learning', in L.A. Hirschfield and S.A. Gelman (eds), *Mapping the Mind: Domain Specificity in Cognition and Culture*. New York: Cambridge University Press, pp. 474–494.

Serre, D. and Wagner, A.C. (2015) 'For a Relational Approach to Cultural Capital: A Concept Tested by Changes in the French Social Space', *The Sociological Review*, 63(2): 433–450.

Silva, E. (2016) 'Unity and Fragmentation of the Habitus', *The Sociological Review*, 64(1): 166–183.

Skeggs, B. (2004) *Class, Self and Culture*. London: Routledge.

Van der Veer, R. and Valsiner, J. (1991) *Understanding Vygotsky: A Quest for Synthesis*. Oxford: Blackwell.

Vygotsky, L.S. (1930) *The Genesis of Higher Psychological Functions*. Moscow: Academy of Pedagogical Sciences.

Vygotsky, L.S. (1978) *Mind in Society*. Cambridge, MA: Harvard University Press.

Vygotsky, L.S. (1981) 'The Development of the Higher Forms of Attention in Childhood', in J.V. Wertsch (ed.), *The Concept of Activity in Soviet Psychology*. Armonk, NY: M.E. Sharpe, pp. 189–240.

Vygotsky, L.S. (1987) *The Collected Works of L.S. Vygotsky. Vol. 1, Problems of General Psychology*. New York: Plenum Press.

Vygotsky, L.S. and Luria, A.R. (1994) *Studies on the History of Behaviour: Ape, Primitive, and Child*. London: Lawrence Erlbaum.

Vuorisalo, M. (2011) 'Children's Resources in Action – the Conversion of Capital in the Pre-school Field', in L. Alanen and M. Siisiäinen (eds), *Fields and Capitals: Constructing Local Life*. University of Jyväskylä, Institute for Educational Research, pp. 29–60.

Vuorisalo, M., Rutanen, N. and Raittila, R. (2015) 'Constructing Relational Space', *Early Years*, 35(1): 1–13.

Wacquant, L. (2014) 'Homines in Extremis: What Fighting Scholars Teach Us about Habitus', *Body and Society*, 20(2): 3–17.

5

YOUNG CHILDREN'S PLAY – CHALLENGING THE ADULT ESTABLISHMENT

Introduction

Play has long been characterised as a defining activity of young children. It is one very important field where we can observe young children developing their own distinctive stocks of cultural and social capital. As directors of their own play-material they are always trying to develop their own separate play culture, and within that, resist adult power and authority. This chapter will argue that young children's play should be framed within a relational context: young children create their own cultural practices through the appropriation of adult-centred discourses, but they do not mimic or passively accept the adult world.

Play can take on many forms but builds on the idea that young children's learning needs to be 'hands-on', enjoyable and self-directed: building with blocks, exploring sand and water, playing pretend, listening to stories, singing and dancing are just a few of the many examples. While many kinds of play can allow such self-expression, pretend play and the production of narratives is considered to be the epicentre of such activity (Paley, 2004) and will therefore be the main focus for our discussion. Pretend play is a key source for young children's intellectual, social and emotional development (Hirsh-Pasek et al., 2009), fostering skills of role rehearsal, self-regulation, turn taking, joint planning and negotiation. As young children use substitute objects in imaginary situations, for example, a broom can become a horse, they become adept at distinguishing symbols from real-life objects. Consequently, they become better able to use words, gestures and other symbols as tools for managing their own behaviour.

I will begin by reviewing the developmental stage theories of play that were proposed by two major developmental psychologists, Jean Piaget and Lev Vygotsky, both of whom were discussed in the previous chapter. Play provides important benefits for learning and developmental processes, as well as for disciplines in curriculum areas (Bodrova, 2008). For Piaget, play is assimilation – young children experiment with different behavioural and cognitive schemas and gain pleasure from the cognitive mastery that stems from self-styled repetition. Vygotsky focused on the role of mediating adults or peers in young children's development – through relationships with such guiding figures, they are led towards a more complex understanding of their world. Play activities are considered to be particularly effective for young children's communicative, narrative and representational competence, through symbolisation and multi-modal forms of expression such as painting, modelling, collage, sculptures and drawing (Carruthers and Worthington, 2011).

We discuss Corsaro's (2003) interpretive approach to play as an alternative to this linear perspective, where young children pass through developmental stages acquiring cognitive and language abilities in preparation for their later adult life. His concept of 'peer culture' is a vital step in overcoming such a narrow instrumental view of play and can help to explain young children's interpretations of their surrounding culture. These interpretations are shaped by their ability to represent the perspective of others and to use objects, body movements, gestures and language. Studies on peer cultures suggest that children, aged three to six years, have a great awareness of their status and roles, with high-status positions able to provide more directives in play than low-status ones (Corsaro, 2005).

A different and more radical interpretation of young children's play is then offered by the German-Jewish philosopher and literary critic, Walter Benjamin (1892–1940). The world of the child was one of the persistent and recurring themes of his writings, yet despite its central importance it is surprising that so little has been written about this aspect of his work (Jessop, 2013). Benjamin made frequent mention of children throughout his essays, and in his *Arcades Project* he wrote about toys and play and children's perception of colour. He also wrote an autobiographical collection of childhood fragments, *Berlin Childhood around 1900* (Benjamin, 2006), and a number of radio broadcasts for young children. A central theme developed in Walter Benjamin's writings about his Berlin childhood and in *One-Way Street* (1997) is the peculiar affinity that young children have with the world of objects encountered in their urban environment. Their playful activities are marked by an intimate connection to and immersion in the surrounding world. For Benjamin, mimesis is a fundamental dimension of play, 'involving the ability to make correspondences by means of spontaneous fantasy' (Buck-Morss, 1991: 263).

Benjamin's perspective is important for further developing a sociology of early childhood because it offers a relational approach for understanding the relationship between Bourdieu's primary and secondary habitus that was discussed in the previous chapter. His writings are an attempt to restore the earliest impressions of childhood which have not yet been tainted by the destructive power of habit. This can provide an important tool for reconnecting in a subtle way with the layers of early childhood experience that have become forgotten, but can nevertheless be recovered.

To understand how some of these aspects of play are enacted from a young child's perspective, I draw on the work of another twentieth-century literary critic, the Russian semiotician Mikhail Bakhtin (1895–1975). His idea of carnival is particularly useful for investigating the imaginative, spontaneous, unpredictable and powerful aspects of pretend play (Cohen, 2011). This concept of the carnival is used to explore the relational dynamics of play which shape young children's relative independence from adults. In a similar way to the carnival, young children try to break down barriers and challenge power inequalities by mocking the hierarchical order established by parents and teachers - they attempt to resist authority and generate disorder to gain more control over their lives.

Play as Learning and Development

During much of the twentieth century, Jean Piaget's theories dominated Western child development research. Piaget (1951) recognised the importance of play for young children, but understood its function mainly as an opportunity to practise newly acquired skills and concepts. Play emerges from the desire to make sense of lived experiences, enabling young children to cope with the confusion that arises in their lives. In Piaget's terms, symbolic play is a form of representational assimilation – young children represent the world according to their understanding and preferences. He emphasised the fantasy aspects of play in pre-school children: the young child assimilates the world to his or her own ego in play, rather than changing his or her own ideas to meet the demands of reality.

The work of another important developmental psychologist, Lev Vygotsky, has also been very influential in our understanding of play. When young children play their attention is more on the *meaning* of things and events in imagined worlds rather than on actual objects. There is a divergence between what a young child actually perceives and the meanings created: in play, thought 'is separated from objects and action arises from ideas rather than from things' (Vygotsky, 1978: 97). A stick may become a sword, a doll a child, a hand represents a person, or a moving boy may create a dragon. Vygotsky (1978: 102) writes that play creates a zone of proximal development for the child where he can act 'as though he were a head taller than himself'. The concept of the Zone of Proximal Development (ZPD) can help us to explain how young children benefit from adult 'scaffolding' of their imagination, pretence and subject knowledge (Vygotsky, 1978). It has been used to study the role of play in cognitive development and can enhance creative practice in a range of areas, such as numeracy, literacy and the arts (Wood and Attfield, 2005).

From their first year young babies have an ability to initiate playful exchanges with their peers. When three 8–12-month-olds in their strollers were left together in a group without an adult present, the infants spontaneously began to reach out to each other with their feet to begin a game of 'footsie' (Selby and Bradley, 2003). As children become more mobile during their second year of life, their play with peers may become more physical and involve 'running, jumping, trampling, twisting, bouncing, romping and shouting, falling ostentatiously, laughing ostentatiously' (Løkken, 2000: 531). It can also involve many affectionate gestures such as gently patting and caressing each other. Toddlers delight in each other's presence and in the play opportunities in familiar, everyday objects. This gives toddlers' play a distinctively joyful quality. By around three to four years old, young children can take great pleasure in playfully and intentionally flouting rules, routines and the expectations of others.

However, this emphasis on development has tended to dominate play research in the early years, with studies relying on Piaget's cognitive developmental theory and Vygotsky's socio-cultural approach (Roskos et al., 2010). In a critical analysis of a set of 20 play-literacy studies published in the last decade (1992–2000), Roskos and Christie (2001: 70) found that although the major claims of 12 of the 20 studies were 'sound, complete, and of scientific value', they had limitations. One weakness was the dominance of Piagetian and Vygotskian theories in the play-literacy research agenda. They found play-literacy studies use these two theoretical frameworks as the 'drivers of research efforts to the near exclusion of other explanatory models' (Roskos and Christie, 2001: 72). Corsaro (2005: 27) has similarly argued that these frameworks have focused primarily on 'developmental outcomes and failed to seriously consider the complexity of social structure and children's collective activities'.

Lester and Russell (2008) have also argued that for the past 30 years attempts at interpreting the benefits of play for young children have been largely instrumental – relying on explanations that see play as serving a specific purpose and outcome. In an extensive literature review on children's play, they found a considerable volume of research that focused on young children's cognitive development and very little material that explored other forms of play, notably those that adults find distasteful or worrying. Young children's play activities were given value only to the extent that they contributed to socially valued aspects of later life or to higher level cognitive functions. But the risk in emphasising 'educational play' is that adults may begin to dominate play, or disguise didactic teaching as support for play. Play then becomes a tool for guiding the development of young children, giving adults licence to determine desirable goals and censure other forms (Brown and Cheeseman, 2003).

A good example of the way that young children's play can be misconstrued and easily dismissed by adults is given by Bruno Bettelheim in his critique of Piaget's child psychology. In response to a four-year-old child who asked him about an elephant's wings, Piaget answered that elephants don't fly. The young girl insisted, 'Yes, they do; I've seen them.' Bettelheim (1991) argues that if Piaget had engaged in conversation about where the elephant needed to fly to in such a hurry, or what dangers he was trying to escape from, then the issues which the young child was grappling with might have emerged, because he would have shown his willingness to accept her way of exploring the problem. He comments that 'This is the tragedy of so much "child psychology": its findings are correct and important, but do not benefit the child. Psychological discoveries aid the adults in comprehending the child from within an adult's frame of reference' (Bettelheim, 1991: 120).

According to Sutton-Smith (1997) this developmental approach is an attempt by adults to organise and control young children's play. He argues that children always seek to have their own separate play culture, and, within that, resistance against adult power and conventions is a hidden transcript of childhood. In the rest of this chapter, we will explore how other theoretical perspectives can expand and deepen play theory, focusing on the work of William Corsaro (2005), Walter Benjamin and Mikhail Bakhtin. An important way of beginning to understand how young children deeply engage with their play is to focus on the rich sources of material that are now available on their peer cultures.

Young Children's Peer Cultures

When young children spend time together over a long period, as they do in pre-school, they develop their own peer cultures. Being a pre-school child means that you are part of a very specific peer culture, holding unique, shared ideas of your own social position and status as well as that of your friends. In her study of pre-school children's play, Löfdahl (2002) found that high-status positions were linked to better chances for carrying on and directing negotiations in play. Making claims on space and objects are ways to take control, though some objects were found to be more valuable than others - props, furniture and different places were 'loaded with status' in various play situations. In contrast to previous research where props were shown to strengthen role characters (Lindqvist, 1995), Löfdahl suggests that props are of less use when young children make their role characters life-like; they would rather use their voices and body movements. Nevertheless, they are aware of the significance props can bring as status symbols. Within their peer cultures young children construct a range of strategies for including and excluding peers, linking status position to social reproduction.

In his theory of interpretive reproduction Corsaro (2003, 2005) argued that children's participation is a process where culturally mediated knowledge is activated as every new generation strives to understand its own meaning in relation to its conditions. Children are both part of cultural production and change as they appropriate information from the adult world and use it in a creative and interpretive way. When groups of young children are the main focus, their participation in a peer culture contributes to their construction of shared social knowledge about being together. Corsaro's theory is important for overcoming the individualistic bias of traditional theories by emphasising the importance of collective action and social structure.

But Gaskins (2014) still asks, 'is play fundamentally individual or social'? Is the goal of pretend play *inventive* self-expression or *interpretive* internalisation of cultural meaning? She argues that a significant theoretical issue that emerges from a consideration of the influence of cultural variation is whether pretend play derives its meaning for young children from the individual expression of their needs and frustrations (inventive play), or through exploration with others of the meaning of social roles and relationships (interpretive play). Pretend play can focus either on narratives that invent unrealistic roles and events (such as going on an adventure to upside-down land or being pirates), or on narratives that interpret realistic ones (such as having breakfast or going to school). In contrast to inventive pretend play, the goal of interpretive pretend play is not self-expression or creativity – it is to understand reality better through enacting events and roles that are within young children's experience.

However, Gaskin's attempt to introduce a distinction in the conceptualisation of pretend play can easily lead to a false dichotomy between an individual child's playing activities and the group to which he or she belongs. Corsaro offers a much more suitable sociological model to explain the relational dynamics which shape relationships between adults and young children and the tensions that stem from their desire for independence from adults and their simultaneous dependence on them. Their peer-play can be studied as reproductive mechanisms that contain a substantial element of jointly constructed interpretations, carried out by young children over time to make sense of their daily lives. Corsaro aptly summarises children's agency in the production and participation of unique peer cultures: 'children are not simply internalizing society and culture, but are actively contributing to cultural production and change' (Corsaro, 2003: 2).

But Guss (2005) argues that Corsaro's influential research on young children's play adheres to a narrow interpretation of the value of play which is too dependent on the interpretive reproduction of experience, where *reproduction* means imitation or copy. In Corsaro's theory, social realistic playing is regarded primarily as a rehearsal for functioning in adult roles later in life: young children imitate behaviour and interpret it simultaneously. However, whereas social realistic playing is imitative of role models, fantasy playing is transformative and often transgressive. While the concept of imitation implies a copy of the original, the concept of mimesis implies a transformation of a model or process of representation. For Guss (2005), it is critical receptivity to an object, a sensuous moment of discovery rather than a reproduction of the original. She argues that the significance of this aesthetic dimension, 'the sensory, sensual, mind–body connection that goes into imagining, forming, and enacting roles and dramatic situations' (Guss, 2005: 234), has been given insufficient attention by sociologists and developmental psychologists. In the rest of this chapter I will draw on the ideas of the German philosopher and literary critic Walter Benjamin to develop an alternative version of play, one that explores the way in which young children's pretence is not simply an imitation of the real world but highly creative and transformative. I will also argue that their pretence can often be highly subversive, using Bakhtin's concept of the carnival to highlight how young children can turn the established adult order on its head.

Walter Benjamin on Childhood

Gershom Scholem, a lifelong friend of Walter Benjamin, drew attention to the significance of children for Benjamin and pointed out how important it was for him to understand the process of remembering his own childhood: 'throughout his life he was attracted with almost magical force by the child's world and ways' (Scholem, 1976: 175). Benjamin wanted to understand the pre-habitual gaze of the young child by retrieving the buried memories of early childhood. He was concerned with the remembrance of young children's perception of things, how they see and experience their world. But Benjamin's aim was not simply to explain the unfolding of young children's activities themselves (Imai, 2003). Through mimetic activities they enter into the world in which adults live; adults, in return, receive the secret signal of what is to come from the gesture of the child (Benjamin, 2005a: 206). It is 'secret' because it comes from the world of young children, a world no longer available to adults; it is a 'signal' because it is sent to the world of adults in the form of visible activities.

Young children play in a world of sensuous correspondence that is in close touch with an archaic, magical mode of relating to things. Within the fragile magic of the home, the child playfully inhabits an enchanted realm of objects, deriving fugitive knowledge from the rattling of the rolled-up window blinds or the swaying of branches that rustle against the house. In 'Toys and Play' Benjamin (2005b: 120) emphasises the importance of repetition for young children's play, explaining its potent desire and intensity:

> We know that for a child repetition is the soul of play, that nothing gives him greater pleasure than to 'Do it again!' ... the child is not satisfied with twice, but wants the same thing again and again, a hundred or even a thousand times. ... Not a 'doing as if' but a 'doing the same thing over and over again,' the transformation of a shattering experience into habit – that is the essence of play.

In the repetition of play, young children repeatedly savour the pleasures that victory offers. Within this process, they have recognised how the environment functions and have gained power over it and themselves. Young children can therefore be understood as directors of their own play-material: they do not stand back and contemplate the object, but take hold of it and, mimetically, become part of it. They possess the mimetic capacity not just for inventive reception, but for active transformation (Gess, 2010). By drawing characters and events into a pattern, so the young child is initiated into the secret life of ordinary objects, often the most miniscule (Eiland, 2006: xiv). In this transformative process, Benjamin (2006) depicts childhood as a blurring of the borders between dream, fantasy and reality. He captures the young child's gift for waiting around, insinuating himself into the keeping of things, masking himself with pieces of furniture: 'the dining table under which he is crouching turns him into the wooden idol in a temple whose four pillars are the carved legs' (Benjamin, 1997: 74).

Young children are also irresistibly drawn to the by-products, the unwanted and discarded objects found in urban landscapes. The old-fashioned and cast-off are rescued and reassembled in miniature. As 'bricoleurs' they take things apart with which they have become intimately familiar, placing them together anew. They discover the 'old world' in its magic, in order, once it is taken apart, to put it together again and thus 'renew' it. For young children, found things are triumphs: as collectors, they rescue disregarded objects and renew them in magical configurations. Collection is an act of renewal, rather than possession. The object, redeemed and renewed, is arranged in new contexts. Through their playfulness, the broken and forgotten object is transformed into something valuable. The demolition site is transformed into a site of playful reconstruction. Gess (2010) argues that this is an incorporative form of destruction – one built on the dialectical transformation of mimesis as constraint to an instrument of self-empowerment, presuming great intimacy with things that are taken apart. Young children have, as a result of their playfulness, a closeness to objects that is later superseded in adulthood by a sense of superiority and a condescending gaze.

Trouble and Taboo

Young children's play has traditionally been dismissed by adults as harmless high-jinks, games in which everyone runs around, giggles, squeals or shouts, arguing over rules or their application. As I previously suggested, the early studies of the effect of play on development were influenced by the emergence and dissemination of constructivist theories of learning (Piaget, 1951; Vygotsky, 1978), leading to an enthusiasm for providing 'playful learning' in both family and pre-school settings. However, the resulting 'play pedagogies' were viewed as Eurocentric with regard to children in the Majority World, where, it was assumed, childhood was a time for work or study rather than for play (Wood, 2009). These traditional conceptions of play reflected the perspectives of Western scholars who have studied the interactions of middle-class European or Euro-American children (Trawick-Smith, 2010). Research on play has thus been too narrow in scope, focusing only on childhood pastimes that are observed within Western societies, whilst undervaluing many significant play forms that are common in non-Western cultures.

Cross-cultural studies have helped to address this Eurocentric approach: Gaskins et al. (2006), for example, have drawn on case studies to support a classification of cultural attitudes to play as 'cultivating' (Euro-American and Taiwanese families), 'accepting' (the Kpelle community in Liberia) or 'curtailing' (a Mayan community in Mexico). In Africa, Mtonga (2012) compiled the texts of indigenous Chewa and Tumbuka children's songs and observed games in rural and urban areas of Zambia. His analysis of guessing games and riddle contests emphasised how these games encouraged young children to think about their own and others' activities – of particular significance were the language games which demonstrated 'playful and skilful manipulation of certain word-sounds in order to distort meaning, create new concepts, or paint a satirical caricature'(Serpell and Nsamenang, 2014).

However, studies of riddles in African contexts have tended to emphasise their role in instilling cultural values (see Kyoore, 2010; Noss, 2006). They discuss the use by adults of riddles – and, in a similar way, other forms of African folklore – as a means of educating and disciplining young children. The social and educational meaning of riddling from the children's perspective and the way these meanings are interpreted in the children's peer culture have to a limited extent been included in the studies of children's folklore. These limitations of the study of the African oral tradition are now being recognised. Jirata (2012), for example, has explored how riddling, a popular form of children's folk culture among the Guji people in Ethiopia, differentiates children's culture from the adult world. She has shown that young children create and share their own cultural practices through which they resist adult imposition. Another good example is the work of Nicolas Argenti (2010), who approaches folktales as child-centred verbal play through which children express their lived experiences; he shows how in the Cameroon grassfields, children - usually so respectful in the presence of elders – revel in the violence and scatological obscenity in which the folktales abound.

In a Western context, children's folklore has been an object of study for over 150 years, with researchers recognising the importance of playground games and clapping and skipping songs. The work of Alice Gomme in 1894 and 1898, which led to the publication of the book *The Traditional Games of England, Scotland and Ireland* (Gomme, 1964), 'did much to establish the study of children's folklore as a valid field of investigation in its own right' (Bishop and Curtis, 2001: 5), while important collections have preserved and protected traditional rhymes and games (Halliwell, 1849), and emphasised the inventiveness and richness of an oral tradition sustained by young children alone (Opie and Opie, 1959, 1969, 1985).

The studies by Opie and Opie have documented thousands of rhymes, clapping rhymes, skipping games, language play, imaginative play and games with rules that are usually referred to as 'childlore'. They were based on information contributed by 20,000 children from schools all over Britain, in response to three surveys, supplemented by the Opies' own in-depth observations and sound recordings. The collection covers a wide range of play and traditions in a variety of outdoor environments – including linguistic items, games, rhymes, songs, customs, rites of passage and beliefs – and provides ethnographic detail on transmission, performance and re-creation. It also allows us to investigate the historical continuities and the continual change through which playground lore responds to contemporary culture, focusing on the power relations of young children's practices (Grugeon, 2001).

Young children's playground games have been investigated from various perspectives as forms of identity and socialisation (James, 1993); as linguistic patterns (Crystal, 1998); as informal literacies (Grugeon, 1988); as musical and compositional practice (Marsh, 2008); and as forms of creative learning (Bishop and Curtis, 2001). But they often gloss over their scatological, obscene and anti-authoritarian nature (Bauman, 1982). Marsh (2008: 171) emphasises the way in which 'parody songs and related parodic movements aptly represent children's subversion of adult culture in their play'. They are often scatological or sexual and publishers in the past have often been reluctant to publish them because of the fear of shocking adults who cannot bear too much reality in a civilised society. Opie (1993: 15) argues that 'defecation, urination, nudity, the private parts, the sex organs, and the sex act have a fearful fascination for children'.

Many funny rhymes are ones which accompany specific game activities, such as counting out, clapping or skipping. Rude variations of Popeye the Sailor Man, for example, accompanied clapping games in the mid-twentieth century. Their humour, their 'cheek', their rhyme and rhythm, imagery, play on words, and frequent parodic traits are all reasons why they appeal to young children and why they are memorable. But the pleasure of the moment seems more important: the opportunity to entertain, make friends laugh, poke fun at authority and benignly insult. Taboos explored by children through verbal play often involve forbidden language and troubling topics such as sex and death. Rhymes dealing with bodily functions, mutilation, sex and death are a perennial feature of playground culture (Roud, 2010).

Carnival and Pretend Role Play

While these parodies of traditional songs and rhymes are not entirely absent from the play of pre-schoolers, their emancipatory potential can sometimes be more evident in activities that directly challenge the propriety of adult customs. Cohen (2011) offers an important illustration of how young children's play sometimes includes imitative elements that border on caricature, satire or a parody of adult roles and behaviours. She uses examples from her study of culturally diverse three- and four-year-olds to identify three main similarities between Bakhtin's ideas about carnival in the Middle Ages and young children's pretence in pre-school classrooms. Bakhtin (1984a) argues that carnival belongs fully to all people and occurs in the public square. In a way very similar to the public square, the dramatic-play area occupies a separate location in the early-childhood classroom, where all children can assume the roles of different characters. It typically contains a kitchen area, a table and chairs, a doll's high chair, a doll bed and dolls representing many cultures. The furniture usually separates the area from the larger classroom. All children in a pre-school programme can participate in dramatic play, which is self-motivated and self-directed, and the area becomes the space where children create a different world within the official world of pre-school.

A second important similarity of carnival and pretend role play resides in the dressing-up and masquerading common in both rituals. In the public square, people used masks and marionettes to take on new identities and overcome fear – to free themselves from the pressures of those with power. Young children use dramatic play in a similar way. They wear hats, scarves and jackets as they take on the roles of mother, father, baby and community workers, and use realistic props, such as telephones, toy food, dishes and stuffed animals as they pretend to eat dinner, celebrate a birthday or work in an office. Through such pretence with clothes and props, young children work out the tensions and paradoxes of the uncertainties of the official adult world that surrounds them (Corsaro, 2005), adapting their voices or their ways of speaking to suit particular roles. Bakhtin (1984b: 185) defines this interaction as 'double-voiced speech', or discourse that is 'directed toward someone else's speech'.

In double-voiced speech, a speaker makes use of another's discourse such that two intentions or speech centres are present in the discourse. Double-voiced discourse occurs when diverse voices interact and struggle to assimilate authoritative discourse (official discourse) and internally persuasive discourse (unofficial discourse). Authoritative discourse is fused with authority and power, located in a distanced zone and connected with a *prior* discourse higher up in the hierarchy. In contrast to authoritative discourse, unofficial or internally persuasive discourse is more flexible and dynamic. With internally persuasive discourse, we appropriate the words of others, redefine them and establish our own voice. According to Bakhtin (1986), each word contains, within itself, diverse, discriminating and often contradictory components. A dialogue thus becomes a model which can be used to explain the emergence and development of group processes.

Cohen (2011: 187–188) provides a good example of double-voiced discourse that is taken from her study of pre-school children. A three-year-old girl role plays her mother attempting to feed her young child hot dogs.

The scene begins as Harry walks over to Sonia who is cooking at the stove.

Sonia to Harry: 'You can't touch this!'

Harry to Sonia: 'Why not?'

(*Sonia cooks and does not answer Harry. Harry gets beaded necklaces from the table and puts them around his neck. He takes food from the basket. Sonia walks over to him.*)

Harry to himself: 'Hot dog, Hot dog!'

(*Harry picks a hot dog out of the basket and asks to eat it.*)

Sonia to Harry: 'Excuse you!'

(*She grabs food away from Harry.*)

Sonia to Harry: 'You can't touch anything.'

(*Sonia delivers her directive in a high-pitched voice and shakes her finger at him.*)

Harry to Sonia: 'What can I have?'

(Harry replies with a low, submissive tone.)

Sonia to Harry: 'Not right now. This is for us!'

(Sonia continues to take food from the food basket and puts items on the plate.

Harry mimics Sonia verbally repeating her and making face gestures.

He continues to pick things out of the basket and attempts to fit them into a frankfurter roll.)

Sonia to Harry: 'Here you go.'

(Sonia puts a food item into a frankfurter roll for him.)

Harry to Sonia: 'Hot dog.'

Sonia to Harry: 'No, that's your fork! And this is your hot dog.'

(Harry leaves the area, and Sonia continues to put food in a pot).

In this example, Sonia and Harry have incorporated adult language directly into their own speech. Sonia takes the authoritative role of Harry's mother. She has assimilated the discourses of her parents and caregivers and repeats and internalises them as her own words. Harry asks for hot dogs, but Sonia uses an authoritative tone to tell him not to begin eating the food. Harry replies submissively to ask his mother what he could eat. After Sonia abruptly responds, employing a demanding high-pitched tone, he mocks her words. Sonia uses dialogue to parody an official parental discourse, while Harry playfully parodies his pretend mother.

Through their parodic exaggeration of adults' discourse, Sonia and Harry enact real-life hierarchies. These parodies bring such discourses and practices into a 'zone of contact' (Bakhtin, 1981: 345) where they are deprived of their absolute authority by the crude and mocking discourse of young children. Here, the contact zone refers to the social space in which adults and young children meet when they engage in discourse that often conflicts. By appropriating an authoritative discourse in pretence, young children develop a sense of identity that helps them contextualise conflict. Through dramatisation, they internalise and redefine the words of others to establish their own voice (Cohen, 2009).

A third similarity between carnival and pretend role play resides in the planning of playful events. Carnival practices, such as underwear becoming outerwear, clothes worn inside out, nose picking and displaying backsides were common during festivals. Participants were able to communicate openly and in ways that exercised freedom from societal constraints through laughter, grotesque acts and profanities. According to Bakhtin (1984a), a key aspect of carnival is *grotesque realism*. Degradation is the dominant element of grotesque realism, which is marked by a lowering of abstract, idealised principles (which are in the head). Much of what constitutes such degradation is associated with the body: drinking and eating for example. In addition to corporal references, grotesque realism consists of discursive features, notably curses, oaths, slang, tricks, jokes and scatological and other forms of folk humour as part of an overall comic ridicule and profanation of authority.

For Bakhtin 'the unofficial carnival is people's second life, organised on the basis of laughter' (1984a: 8), which has the 'power of making an object come up close, of drawing it into a zone of crude contact where one can finger it familiarly on all sides, turn it upside down, inside out, and peer at it from above' (Bakhtin, 1981: 23). Carnival is a way of breaking down barriers, of overcoming power inequalities through the playful mockery of hierarchical order by individuals oppressed by it. Similar to the carnival, young children are placed in an official hierarchy that subjects them to the demands of parents and teachers – they escape official channels, resist authority and generate disorder to gain control of their lives (Corsaro, 2005).

However White (2014) argues that there are unique pedagogical challenges for teachers in recognising the pedagogic value of young children's carnivalesque humour that is typically tolerated, corrected or ignored rather than viewed as an opportunity for engagement (Smeed, 2011). Early years teachers need to position themselves both horizontally and vertically: the former position recognises one's role as integral to the humour that takes place (as an authorial partner, one is willing to become the object of ridicule, to potentially becomes the butt of the joke); while the latter demands a stepping away from the role as 'expert' to one of dialogic uncertainty which recognises that the carnivalesque lies within the domain of the peer group. Embracing both these roles is potentially transformative and ensures that the carnivalesque can thrive as a major way of engaging with young children.

Young Children's Humour

Despite a considerable volume of psychological-based research investigating the pedagogical prominence of young children's humour (see, for example, Loizou, 2007), it has not enjoyed the attention it warrants within early childhood research. Of the wide range of studies of humour in education over the last four decades, few have explored humour within early childhood, focusing instead on school-aged children (Banas et al., 2011). However, there are notable exceptions – recent New Zealand assessment based on Kaupapa Maaori ideology highlights the significance of adults' recognition of and engagement with young children's humour (Ministry of Education, 2009). Drawing on the metaphor of Maui-tika-tika-a-Tauranga (a character from a popular legend), teachers are encouraged to value humour as a disposition which privileges the notion of whakatoi/whakataka – described by Rameka (2009: 35) as 'cheekiness, spiritedness, displaying and enjoying humour, having fun'.

A small number of studies have also explored the social aspect of engagement as a key to understanding young children's humour in early childhood. Loizou's (2007) investigation of 18- and 21-month-old children provides several examples of their deliberate employment of mismatching in order to generate a reaction from others. Such incongruity was evident in the violation of rules, misnaming of items, misuse of materials and even, in the case of the 21-month-old, the telling of 'knock-knock' jokes. Much of this humour was directed towards the teacher and sought a reaction in response, even if it was a negative one. Such humour 'is a social and playful activity that can be a catalyst for the development of social knowledge and lead to the understanding of one's self as a social agent, early on' (Loizou, 2007: 204).

Loizou (2005) also explored how six 1–2-year-old children in group child care demonstrated their ability to appreciate and produce humour. She defines humour as the ability to empower oneself by playfully violating or appreciating the violation of someone's expectations and responding through smiles or laughter. Many of the humorous events were intentionally produced by young children as an attempt to violate their peers' or caregivers' expectations in order to make themselves feel superior to their caregivers. For example, instead of using the sponge to clean their space, some children would put it in their mouth, look up at their caregiver and smile, knowing and understanding their action and implications. This was a favourite activity, and once one child started the rest followed. They produced and sometimes appreciated similar events by watching their peers put the sponge in their mouths:

> Calvin is sitting at the table. Amy [caregiver] gives him a sponge and asks him to clean up his space. He puts the sponge on his head, stops, and looks at Amy. Amy looks at him and smiles. She gets the sponge and asks him if he thinks the sponge is a hat. He says, 'yeah' and smiles. Then Amy asks him if he thinks he is a funny boy and he says, 'yeah' smiling. (Loizou, 2005: 50)

Humour is therefore important because it allows young children to challenge adult power, explore taboo topics such as sex or toilets and to experiment with dazzling displays of verbal dexterity. They are able to exercise an element of control over their underground world by finding opportunities to engage in humour that explores forbidden territory. Tallant (2015) argues that young children can debase adult authority by engaging with imagery that dominant cultural discourses claim as inappropriate, relishing the power they have over their own bodies. This may be a particularly enjoyable experience because children aged three and four may have only recently become toilet-trained and gained control over their bladders and bowels.

When young children play, they engage in a form of 'rebellion – the thwarting of more powerful others – as well as attempts at control of and letting go of restraints' (Henricks, 2009: 29). They are viewed as uncivilised in their purportedly 'closer' connection to unregulated emotions, senses and the body (Howes, 2005). As a participant observer in an early childhood setting in West London, Rosen (2015) provides a good example of the way that young children can sometimes challenge attempts to manage and control their emotions. In her research she discusses three critical moments involving screams, arguing that they came to be seen as an aspect of voice quality that must be managed, controlled and regulated during imaginative play.

She observed that whilst a group of young children were playing dragons a collective scream suddenly emerged. This unintentional scream had the consequence of opening up a space for something new, raising questions about the existing 'order' of the early childhood setting. With the magnitude of the sound produced in this moment there was a particular distortion which took place: the strange sensation of producing a voice from inside the individual body and having a similar type of sound return and surround the body in amplified form. Such sonic intensity as well as ambiguity – the complex effects on the young children's bodies brought about by the indeterminacy of where one voice started and another stopped – created a group amplification of emotions and embodied intensities.

Rosen (2015) suggests that this collective scream offered children a momentary release from a much-prized calm, quiet and orderly nursery. Significantly, this disordered use of the scream, in terms of the play narrative and expectations within the setting, created a sense of community. The physical reverberations and the all-encompassing nature of the scream were important factors in drawing these dragon-children together, many of whom had often made use of individual screams with more antagonistic meanings in narrative or in real conflict with each other. But at the same time as this scream brought about community, it also excluded those who did not or could not join in: those children who sat down quietly or backed away as the scream rose in decibels. Their withdrawal may have been a response to self-imposed social conventions regarding 'appropriate' vocalisations in early years settings or physical reactions to the scale of the sound.

Conclusions

This chapter began by reviewing some of the influential psychological approaches to young children's play as represented by two of the most important developmental psychologists of the twentieth century, Jean Piaget and Lev Vygotsky. For Piaget, the young child is considered to have appropriately adapted to the environment when he or she has achieved a balance between accommodation – adjustment to uncooperative circumstances – and assimilation – the manipulation of these circumstances. He considers young children's play as a non-serious, trivial activity, diverting fun or fantasy that deflects from the later development of adult rationality. I argued that in treating play from the perspective of the rational and serious adult, Piaget is specifically under-valuing an important aspect of young children's playful activities (Jenks, 2008). The rhetorics of play as 'progress' or 'growth', promoted within developmental psychology and education is one of the most important ways of inscribing the irrational aspects of play with 'rational' attributes (Sutton-Smith, 1997).

Vygotsky identified play as the leading activity for cognitive development during the pre-school years. Play activity, according to Vygotsky (1978), creates a zone of proximal development for pre-schoolers; it affords us a glimpse of young children's future achievements and enables them to act in ways that are in advance of their real-life actions. By drawing the young child into extensive imitation and reconstruction of adult activities, play activity leads the child forward in development. However, through their play young children do not simply reproduce aspects of adult life, but are involved in creative processes where real situations can take on new and unfamiliar meanings: their play activity 'is not simply a recollection of past experience, but a creative reworking' of it (Vygotsky, 1990: 87).

One important way of exploring this 'creative reworking' of adult culture is to examine the position of young children within their peer cultures, where they take charge and control of themselves. According to Corsaro (2003: 112), the 'appropriation and embellishment of adult models is about status, power, and control'. Whereas adults exchange thoughts verbally, young children enter the play-arena and converse within dramatic languages and structures, creating a dramaturgy where they have the space and liberty to take control, to represent and transform their imaginations. In transformational play, young children's forms of dramatic representations can be viewed as radical interventions in what they have experienced (Guss, 2005).

I then looked at the transformative and mimetic aspects of young children's play by discussing the alternative perspectives of Walter Benjamin and Mikhail Bakhtin, arguing that both can be used to deepen our relational understanding of play. In representing the experiences of childhood Benjamin was aware of the dangers inherent in writing about the past as an adult. But unlike Piaget, Benjamin was not interested in the sequential development of stages of abstract, formal reason, but in what was lost along the way. His aim was to reconnect the world of the adult and the young child by uncovering young children's alternative modes of seeing and knowing. For Benjamin, the task of memory is to uncover this relational space, retrieving the buried hopes, aspirations and dreams of young children that have become frustrated during the course of adulthood.

Bakhtin's view of the carnivalesque can be very helpful here for exploring in greater depth how young children perceive their worlds. In dramatic play they undermine and transgress the authoritative discourses of adults: knowing what characters do or might do, they use their words, objects, actions and ideas to take control of events. The 'contact zone' in dramatic play forms the social space that allows adults and young children to meet and engage in discourses that often conflict. This social space enables young children to develop a sense of self, positioning themselves in relation to other speakers and viewpoints. Thus, by appropriating and changing character roles, they learn about the points of view of other people and expand their own concepts. The construction of such relational spaces is intimately connected with the important problem of social control, which we will explore in the next chapter by looking at long-term developments in the relation between young children and their parents.

DISCUSSION ACTIVITY

Childhood is the world of miracle or of magic: it is as if creation rose luminously out of the night, all new and fresh and astonishing. Childhood is over the moment things are no longer astonishing. When the world gives

(Continued)

(Continued)

you a feeling of 'déjà vu,' when you are used to existence, you become an adult. (Ionesco, 1998)

1. What do you remember about your favourite toy or game as a young child – how did it conjure up magic moments?
2. Explore the relationship between time and place in some of your early childhood memories?
3. When adults become too familiar with the world, do they lose their childhood curiosity?

Further Reading

Wendy Russell (2012) '"I Get Such a Feeling out of... Those Moments": Playwork, Passion, Politics and Space', *International Journal of Play*, 1(1): 51–63.

This paper offers an unusual approach to play by applying the spatial analyses of the French Marxist Henri Lefebvre. Wendy Russell explores the way that UK playworkers, who mainly work with school-aged children in a wide range of settings including adventure playgrounds, play centres and out of school care schemes, discuss the purpose of their work. Even though her analysis highlights the continued dominance of psychology and rational approaches to intervention in children's lives, she shows that children still have spaces to resist and rearrange their own worlds.

The 'Childhoods and Play' Project

From the 1950s to the 1980s, Iona and Peter Opie conducted surveys of children's play and folklore, which they published in a series of landmark texts, for example, *The Lore and Language of School Children* (Opie and Opie, 1959). Some 20,000 children from schools across England, Scotland and Wales sent letters and drawings to the Opies, documenting their play, language games and folklore. This project aims to digitise this internationally significant collection, making it freely available to all for academic, educational and community purposes. You can find out further information about the project and some of its useful resources at the website, www.opieproject.group.shef.ac.uk

Jane Read (2011) 'Gutter to Garden: Historical Discourses of Risk in Interventions in Working Class Children's Street Play', *Children and Society*, 25(6): 421–434.

Jane Read provides an illuminating historical perspective that identifies continuities and discontinuities about suitable play spaces for young children. She investigates the implementation of strategies in the first decade of the twentieth century to relocate the 'gutter' play of British working-class children from the street to free kindergartens, arguing that this type of play served as a powerful metaphor for filth and therefore embodied a threat to young children and society. The materials and sensory experiences of young children's own environment were construed as 'dirty' or 'dangerous', whilst the positive benefits of street play, their imaginative and creative potential, were incorporated within morally improving discourses that embodied romantic conceptions of appropriate activities for young children's development.

References

Argenti, N. (2010) 'Things That Don't Come by the Road: Folktales, Fosterage, and Memories of Slavery in the Cameroon Grassfields', *Comparative Studies in Society and History*, 52(2): 224–254.

Bakhtin, M.M. (1981) *The Dialogic Imagination*. Austin: University of Texas Press.

Bakhtin, M.M. (1984a) *Rabelais and His World*. Bloomington: Indiana University Press.

Bakhtin, M.M. (1984b) *Problems of Dostoevsky's Poetics*. Minneapolis: University of Minnesota Press.

Bakhtin, M.M. (1986) *Speech Genres and Other Late Essays*. Austin: University of Texas.

Banas, J.A., Dunbar, N., Rodriguez, D. and Liu, S. (2011) 'A Review of Humour in Educational Settings: Four Decades of Research', *Communication Education*, 60(1): 115–144.

Bauman, R. (1982) 'Ethnography of Children's Folklore', in P. Gilmore and A. Glatthorn (eds), *Children In and Out of School*. Washington, DC: Center for Applied Linguistics, pp. 172–186.

Benjamin, W. (1997) *One-Way Street*. London: Verso.

Benjamin, W. (2005a) 'Program for a Proletarian Children's Theater', in *Walter Benjamin: Selected Writings, Volume 2, Part 1, 1927–1930*. Cambridge: Belknap Press, pp. 201–206.

Benjamin, W. (2005b) 'Toys and Play: Marginal Notes on a Monumental Work', in *Walter Benjamin: Selected Writings, Volume 2, Part 1, 1927–1930*. Cambridge: Belknap Press, pp. 117–121.

Benjamin, W. (2006) *Berlin Childhood around 1900*. Cambridge: Belknap Press.

Bettelheim, B. (1991) *The Uses of Enchantment: The Meaning and Importance of Fairy Tales*. London: Penguin.

Bishop, J.C. and Curtis, M. (2001) 'Introduction', in J.C. Bishop and M. Curtis (eds), *Play Today in the Primary School Playground: Life, Learning and Creativity*. Buckingham: Open University Press, pp. 1–19.

Bodrova, E. (2008) 'Make-believe Play Versus Academic Skills: A Vygotskian Approach to Today's Dilemma of Early Childhood Education', *European Early Childhood Education Research Journal*, 16(3): 357–369.

Brown, F. and Cheeseman, B. (2003) 'Introduction: Childhood and Play', in F. Brown (ed.), *Playwork Theory and Practice*. Maidenhead: Open University, pp. 1–6.

Buck-Morss, S. (1991) *The Dialectics of Seeing: Walter Benjamin and the Arcades Project*. Cambridge, MA: MIT Press.

Carruthers, E. and Worthington, M. (2011) *Understanding Children's Mathematical Graphics: Beginnings in Play*. Maidenhead: McGraw Hill Open University Press.

Cohen, L.E. (2009) 'The Heteroglossic World of Preschoolers' Pretend Play', *Contemporary Issues in Early Childhood*, 10(4): 331–342.

Cohen, L.E. (2011) 'Bakhtin's Carnival and Pretend Role Play: A Comparison of Social Contexts', *American Journal of Play*, 4(2): 176–202.

Corsaro, W. (2003) *We're Friends, Right? Inside Kids' Culture*. Washington, DC: Joseph Henry Press.

Corsaro, W. (2005) *The Sociology of Childhood*, 2nd edition. Thousand Oaks, CA: Pine Forge Press.

Crystal, D. (1998) *Language Play*. London: Penguin.

Eiland, H. (2006) 'Translator's Foreword', in W. Benjamin, *Berlin Childhood around 1900*. Cambridge: Belknap Press, pp. vii–xvi.

Gaskins, S. (2014) 'Children's Play as Cultural Activity', in E. Brooker, M. Blaise and S. Edwards (eds), *Sage Handbook of Play and Learning in Early Childhood*. London: Sage, pp. 31–42.

Gaskins, S., Haight, W. and Lancey, D. (2006) 'The Cultural Construction of Play', in A. Göncü and S. Gaskins (eds), *Play and Development: Evolutionary, Sociocultural and Functional Perspectives*. Mahwah, NJ, Lawrence Erlbaum Associates, pp. 179–202.

Gess, N. (2010) 'Gaining Sovereignty: On the Figure of the Child in Walter Benjamin's Writing', *MLN*, 125(3): 682–708.

Gomme, A.B. (1964 [1894/1898]) *The Traditional Games of England, Scotland and Ireland: With Tunes, Singing Rhymes, and Methods of Playing According to the Variants Extant and Recorded in Different Parts of the Kingdom*. New York: Dover.

Grugeon, E. (1988) 'Underground Knowledge: What the Opies Missed', *English in Education*, 22(2): 9–17.

Grugeon, E. (2001) '"We Like Singing the Spice Girl Songs … and We Like Tig and Stuck in the Mud": Girls' Traditional Games on Two Playgrounds', in J. Bishop and M. Curtis (eds), *Play Today in the Primary School Playground*. Buckingham: Open University Press, pp. 98–114.

Guss, F. (2005) 'Reconceptualising Play: Aesthetic Self-definitions', *Contemporary Issues in Early Childhood*, 6(3): 233–243.

Halliwell, J.O. (1849) *Popular Rhymes and Nursery Tales*. London: John Russell Smith.

Henricks, T.S. (2009) 'Orderly and Disorderly Play: A Comparison', *American Journal of Play*, 2(1): 12–40.

Hirsh-Pasek, K., Golinkoff, R.M., Berk, L.E. and Singer, D.G. (2009) *A Mandate for Playful Learning in Preschool: Presenting the Evidence*. New York: Oxford University Press.

Howes, D. (2005) 'Introduction: Empires of the Senses', in D. Howes (ed.), *Empire of the Senses: The Sensual Culture Reader*. Oxford: Berg Publishers, pp. 1–17.

Imai, Y. (2003) 'Walter Benjamin and John Dewey: The Structure of Difference between their Thoughts on Education', *Journal of Philosophy of Education*, 37(1): 109–125.

Ionesco, E. (1998) *Present Past, Past Present: A Personal Memoir*. New York: Perseus.

James, A. (1993) *Childhood Identities: Self and Social Relationships in the Experience of the Child*. Edinburgh: Edinburgh University Press.

Jenks, C. (2008) 'Constructing Childhood Sociologically', in M.J. Kehily (ed.), *An Introduction to Childhood Studies*. Maidenhead: Open University and McGraw-Hill, pp. 93–111.

Jessop, S. (2013) 'Children, Redemption and Remembrance in Walter Benjamin', *Journal of Philosophy of Education*, 47(4): 642–657.

Jirata, T.J. (2012) 'Learning through Play: An Ethnographic Study of Children's Riddling in Ethiopia', *Africa*, 82(2): 272–286.

Kyoore, P.K.S. (2010) 'A Study of Riddles among the Dagara of Ghana and Burkina Faso', *Journal of Dagaare Studies*, 7(10): 21–40.

Lester, S. and Russell, W. (2008) *Play for a Change – Play, Policy and Practice: A Review of Contemporary Perspectives*. London: National Children's Bureau.

Lindqvist, G. (1995) *The Aesthetics of Play: A Didactic Study of Play and Culture in Preschools*. Uppsala: Acta Universitatis Upsalensis.

Löfdahl, A. (2002) *Förskolebarns lek – en arena för kulturellt och socialt meningsskapande [Pre-school Children's Play – Arenas for Cultural and Social Meaning-making]*. Karlstad University Studies, Karlstad.

Loizou, E. (2005) 'Infant Humor: The Theory of the Absurd and the Empowerment Theory', *International Journal of Early Years Education*, 13(1): 43–53.

Loizou, E. (2007) 'Humour as a Means of Regulating One's Social Self: Two Infants with Unique Humorous Personas', *Early Childhood Development and Care*, 177(2): 195–205.

Løkken, G. (2000) 'The Playful Quality of the Toddling "style"', *International Journal of Qualitative Studies in Education*, 13(5): 531–542.

Marsh, K. (2008) *The Musical Playground: Global Tradition and Change in Children's Songs and Games*. Oxford: Oxford University Press.

Ministry of Education (2009) *Te Whatu Pokeka: Kaupapa Maori Assessment for Learning*. Wellington: Learning Media.

Mtonga, M. (2012) *Children's Games and Plays in Zambia*. Lusaka: University of Zambia.

Noss, P.A. (2006) 'Gbaya Riddles in Changing Times', *Research in African Literatures*, 37(2): 34–42.

Opie, I. (1993) *The People in the Playground*. Oxford: Oxford University Press.

Opie, I. and Opie, P. (1959) *The Lore and Language of Schoolchildren*. Oxford: Oxford University Press.

Opie, I. and Opie, P. (1969) *Children's Games in Street and Playground: Chasing, Catching, Seeking, Vol. 1*. Oxford: Clarendon Press.

Opie, I. and Opie, P. (1985) *The Singing Game*. Oxford: Oxford University Press.

Paley, V.G. (2004) *A Child's Work: The Importance of Fantasy Play*. Chicago, IL: University of Chicago Press.

Piaget, J. (1951) *Play, Dreams and Imitation in Childhood*. London: Heinemann.

Rameka, L. (2009) 'Kaupapa Maaori Assessment: A Journey of Meaning Making', *Early Childhood Folio*, 13: 32–37.

Rosen, R. (2015) '"The Scream": Meanings and Excesses in Early Childhood Settings', *Childhood*, 22(1): 39–52.

Roskos, K. and Christie, J. (2001) 'Examining the Play-Literacy Interface: A Critical Review and Future Directions', *Journal of Early Childhood Literacy*, 1(1): 59–89.

Roskos, K.A., Christie, J.F., Widman, S. and Holding, A. (2010) 'Three Decades In: Priming for Meta-analysis in Play-Literacy Research', *Journal of Early Childhood Literacy*, 10(1): 55–96.

Roud, S. (2010) *The Lore of the Playground*. London: Random House.

Scholem, G. (1976) 'Walter Benjamin', in W.J. Dannhauser (ed.), *On Jews and Judaism in Crisis: Selected Essays*. New York: Schocken Books, pp. 172–197.

Selby, J.M. and Bradley, B.S. (2003) 'Infants in Groups: A Paradigm for the Study of Early Social Experience', *Human Development*, 46(4): 197–221.

Serpell, R. and Nsamenang, A.B. (2014) 'Locally relevant and quality ECCE programmes: Implications of research on indigenous African child development and socialization', UNESCO Early Childhood Care and Education (ECCE) Working Papers Series, 3, Paris: UNESCO.

Smeed, J. (2011) 'Nonsense in the Early Childhood Curriculum', New Zealand Tertiary College Conference: Reaffirming complexity in ECE, November 4, Auckland.

Sutton-Smith, B. (1997) *The Ambiguity of Play*. Cambridge, MA: Harvard University Press.

Tallant, L. (2015) 'Framing Young Children's Humour and Practitioner Responses to it Using a Bakhtinian Carnivalesque Lens', *International Journal of Early Childhood*, 47(2): 251–266.

Trawick-Smith, J. (2010) *Early Childhood Development: A Multicultural Perspective*. Columbus, OH: Merrill.

Vygotsky, L.S. (1978) *Mind in Society: The Development of Higher Psychological Processes*. Cambridge, MA: Harvard University Press.

Vygotsky, L.S. (1990) 'Imagination and Creativity in Childhood', *Soviet Psychology*, 28(1): 84–96.

White, E.J. (2014) '"Are you 'avin a laff?": A Pedagogical Response to Bakhtinian Carnivalesque in Early Childhood Education', *Educational Philosophy & Theory*, 46(8): 898–913.

Wood, E. (2009) 'Conceptualising a Pedagogy of Play: International Perspectives from Theory, Policy and Practice', in D. Kuschner (ed.), *From Children to Red Hatters: Diverse Images and Issues of Play. Play and Culture Studies, Vol. 8*. Maryland: University Press of America, pp. 166–189.

Wood, E. and Attfield, J. (2005) *Play, Learning and the Early Childhood Curriculum*, 2nd edition. London: Paul Chapman.

6

CIVILISING YOUNG CHILDREN – LONG-TERM PARENTING TRENDS

Introduction

In the twenty-first century media commentary and discourses on contemporary childhood commonly invoke a notion of 'crisis' (Furedi, 2008; Hardyment, 2007; Palmer, 2006), fuelled by debates about changes in family structure and the growing attention to parenting from a broad range of professionals. Concern for these parenting issues is informed by very different sources: research centres like The Centre for Parenting Culture Studies at the University of Kent, self-help books, newspaper articles, TV programmes, magazines, websites, podcasts, laws, policy documents, parent training programmes and websites for parents such as Netmums. Parenting in contemporary times, according to Furedi (2008), is imbued with feelings of fear and paranoia.

An obvious manifestation of paranoid parenting can be seen in parents' approach to child safety, an issue that has escalated from a concern to a national obsession. Furedi gives the example of a mother who drove behind the school coach to ensure that her son arrived safely at his destination. He suggests that there is now a heighted sense of anxiety, a 'plague' of paranoid parenting which can be explained by wider cultural forces such as the loss of parental authority and a pervasive sense of young children being under threat and/or out of control. With the publication of his *Paranoid Parenting* (2008), Furedi's work became very influential not only for diagnosing parents' alleged predicament, but for enabling parents to gain some insight into the cultural mechanisms that are responsible for their lack of confidence.

In this chapter I argue that Furedi's analysis of the parenting crisis in contemporary families tends to be focused on short-term developments that need to be explained by long-term relational processes, based on changes in the balance of power between men, women and young children. According to Elias (2008), these changes should be explained by a longer trend of informalisation that has occurred from the late twentieth century onwards. This concept of informalisation refers to a period of movement from an authoritarian to a more egalitarian parent–child relationship where there is a loosening of barriers of authority in relations between young children and adults. In his essay 'The Civilising of Parents' Elias (2008) argued that during the late twentieth century, the parent–child relationship had lost some of its hierarchical character: although young children have greater autonomy in their relationships with adults, both adults and young children are now expected to exercise a higher degree of self-restraint. An important long-term, unintended consequence of this process is that young children and parents live within families in highly interdependent relationships, where there are increasing pressures to control and regulate one's emotions and behaviour.

We then explore how the concept of 'nature' has been used to inform and shape different beliefs and practices about the best way for parents to bring up young children, tracing its emergence to the 'natural education' proposed by Rousseau in *Emile*. These different practices can be understood as major shifts in parental advice, emphasising changing attitudes in the relation between early childhood and adulthood. I will focus on how the child as 'natural', 'pure' and 'innocent' functioned as a basis for the late eighteenth and early nineteenth-century Romantic vision of childhood. The early Romantics believed that to grow up into adulthood and 'civilised' society was a journey away from the source that was the most valuable aspects of ourselves – the child as vital, full of energy and passionate. This 'inner childhood' became a very important touchstone for later scientific and moralistic developments in childrearing practices, because it was based upon the division between the 'good' and 'bad' child. If young children were 'naturally' good, then parents would have to develop skills to meet their needs and educate them. But if they were 'naturally' bad or sinful, then they risked being damned forever.

Changing Family Relationships

When I started my degree in social sciences in the late 1970s at Paisley College near Glasgow, a major topic for discussion on a first-year sociology course was how we could explain the emergence of the nuclear family from extended family networks. As students, we studied a well-known text by Young and Wilmott (1957) on changing family patterns in Britain. Their study highlighted the weakening of kinship networks as young members of the family moved from working-class communities in Bethnal Green in East London to housing estates in Greenleigh in outer London. The caring arrangements of the extended family were threatened by change as the nuclear family became more dominant:

> In a three-generation family the burden of caring for the young as well, though bound to fall primarily on the mothers, can be lightened by being shared with the grandmothers. The three generations complement each other. Once prise out two of them, and the wives are left without the help of grandmothers, the old without the comfort of children and grandchildren. (Young and Wilmott, 1957: 197)

But family relationships have significantly changed in the last 40 years in the UK. The ideal image of the nuclear family, consisting of a white, heterosexual co-residential married couple with their children who are economically supported by a husband, no longer fits with the rich diversity of ways in which family members live their lives. In the twenty-first century, there is no longer one dominant family form that could provide a model for all others. Family structures are changing through divorce, separations or re-partnering and evolving in relation to employment patterns, shifting power balances between men and women and increasing acceptance of choices in sexual orientation. A greater diversity of lifestyles has brought about new opportunities for resources that parents can draw on for support. With the growing trend towards more men and women employed full-time in the workforce, a range of professionals have to be employed to care for many of our young children. National governments are increasingly concerned with the professionalisation of a young children's workforce, leading to heated debates about how to best provide high quality education and care for young children.

Gabb and Silva (2011) have outlined three main strands of thinking which have been particularly influential for explaining these changes in family relationships. The first of these was coined by Morgan (2011) in the phrase 'family practices', which refers to the various expectations and obligations associated with parenthood, partnership and kinship. The second strand is based upon the concept of intimacy (Jamieson, 2011) and refers to familiarity acquired by close association and sharing of detailed knowledge. The third and most recent strand is encapsulated in the concept of 'personal life', where relationships and intimacies are investigated through their interconnections with changing notions of time and politics (see Smart, 2007).

All these strands distance themselves from the concept of 'the family', highlighting the relational aspects of family relationships and the ways in which these relationships are lived and seen. The concept of family has been said to have become decentred, especially in research that draws from broader notions of intimacy and personal life (Edwards and Gillies, 2012; Gillies, 2011). However, Ribbens McCarthy (2012) has forcefully argued that such a methodological focus on personal narratives and life histories might obscure a focus on 'relationships and relationality'. She contends that researchers should be more sensitive to people's everyday discourses of family, the 'language of family' that provides insights into the interweaving of autonomy and connection in the context of close-knit relationships that persist over time. The use of such language acts as 'a repository and expression for deep but ambivalent desire for – and sometimes, fears of – belonging and connection (Ribbens McCarthy, 2012: 70).

Re-positioning Family

However, these different strands in our understanding of changing family relationships also need to be reconsidered in relation to wider processes of state intervention. As I argued in the Introduction there has been an emphasis on investing in young children and on regulating their upbringing and behaviour (for example through parenting orders and fining or jailing parents for child truancy) (Lister, 2006a). Statham and Smith (2010: 17) identify three different but related approaches to early years, interventions: early years' interventions which can target the pre-natal period or young children of any pre-school age; early identification of problems and additional needs; and earlier delivery of services and interventions aimed at promoting resilience among groups at risk of poor outcomes. Programmes for early interventions vary in their primary aims, focusing on, for example, health, early literacy, childcare, family support and parenting. One of the key features of this social policy strategy was to make a link between the reform of the welfare system and the development of a criminal justice agenda dealing with dysfunctional families, anti-social behaviour in children and early intervention to rescue the ill-disciplined 'feral children' in housing estates and poor inner cities (Rodger, 2012).

Such policy changes have been theorised as shifts towards the 'enabling state' (Blair, 1998), the 'social investment' state (Lister, 2006b) or the 'preventive-surveillance' state (Parton, 2006) and have been referred to under a range of different terms – improving child welfare, supporting families, regenerating communities, promoting children's rights to protection, participation and provision, reducing high-cost social problems, promoting resilience, improving the cost-effectiveness of children's services and reducing the need for costly remedial interventions (Churchill, 2011). This 'interventionist agenda' is underpinned by an approach to social exclusion which posits families as the building blocks of society where young children should be taught how to behave. The family has therefore come to be equated with the everyday minutiae of family life, with parenting practices reconfigured as a 'job' that has 'outcomes' for young children. Parenting in this context is not regarded as a behaviour guided by love and experience, but a skilled job in which amateur parents need professional advice (Gillies, 2008).

This repositioning of family life has resulted in a 'professionalisation' of childrearing, seen in terms of a set of complex activities that need to be taught to parents by experts (Ramaekers and Suissa, 2011). Furedi (2008) offers a sharp analysis of the predicament parents find themselves in where they cannot escape the predominant culture of 'paranoid parenting', a parental condition where the distinctive feature is *a lack of confidence* (1) of parents in themselves, (2) of parents in other adults and (3) of policy makers and experts towards parents. This paranoia leads to over-parenting and parent-blaming. Paranoid parenting is not about parents, but involves *a culture* of paranoid parenting:

> It is a culture that dramatizes every issue facing mothers and fathers and turns everyday problems into scare stories. It is also a culture that denigrates parental competence and insists that mothers and fathers cannot cope without the help of experts. These cultural messages are zealously promoted by a formidable network of professional experts, child rearing gurus, child protection advocates, fear entrepreneurs and politicians. (Furedi, 2008: 16)

However, Furedi's culture of paranoid parenting can be better explained by a longer process of informalisation that has occurred from the twentieth century onwards. According to Elias (2008), informalisation has occurred in the context of a 'tightening of the prohibition of the use of physical violence in family life', which 'applies not only to the relations between adults and children within the family, but also applies in the relations between adults and children in general, particularly to those of teachers and children at school' (Elias, 2008: 35). This trend of informalisation, part of the historical development of processes of civilisation, has had a dual impact on childhood: first, the distance between childhood and adulthood gradually increases as the requirements of societal membership become more demanding, so that childhood requires more time and effort in socialisation and education prior to the achievement of adult status through entry to the workforce. Second, adults' investment of time, skill, effort and emotions in young children also increases, making them both more 'precious' and demanding at the same time.

Young children therefore occupy a highly ambivalent place in the lives of parents. On the one hand, they are regarded as costing time, effort and money. On his or her birth, writes Beck (1992: 118), 'the child develops and perfects its "dictatorship of neediness" and forces its biological rhythm of life on its parents through the naked power of its vocal chords and the warmth of its smile'. Yet, on the other hand, these very demands make young children more and more important, 'the source of the last remaining, irrevocable, unexchangeable primary relationship' (Beck, 1992: 118).

Shifts in Parenting Practices

Elias (2008) explains this ambivalence in terms of a long-term trend in adult–child relations, establishing their connection with other developments such as an increasing concern with child abuse and neglect, the tendency towards reducing and eliminating violence from relations with young children, the shift towards seeing children as citizens with rights and a gradual democratisation of adult–child relations. A modified authority relationship between adults and young children 'now really demands of parents … a relatively high degree of self-control, which as a model and a means of education then rebounds to impose a high degree of self-restraint on children in their turn' (Elias, 2008: 37). Significantly, a similar change has occurred in the balance of power in the relations between men and women, as women have become an integral part of the workforce. Men are now expected to become more involved with the care and education of young children and parents are under pressure to renounce violence as a means of discipline.

The focus on contemporary parents to give their young children the best start in life by providing affection and love at home can be seen as part of the process of individualisation (Beck and Beck-Gernsheim, 2002), a marked shift to emotionally intense, child-centred parenting in which the social distance between parents and young children has been reduced. Traditional authoritarian models of family life have given way to more open and democratic parent–child relationships in which rules, relationships and respect are negotiated and worked on together, rather than laid down by adults. Hollway (2006) suggests that 'good' parenthood is evaluated in terms of individual emotional capacity to care and competence to develop opportunities for young children, including knowing what is best for each child according to his or her different character and needs. This principle of parental responsibility for young children's present and future well-being means that anxiety about doing the 'right thing' is at the centre of contemporary experiences of intimate family relationships. As such, many of the so-called 'private' aspects of family life have become subject to advice from a range of experts, including educationalists and childrearing gurus, creating a framework of public expectations about how family life ought to be lived (Plummer, 2003).

According to van Daalen (2010) tensions and anxieties between the private and the public is one of the major issues in the raising of young children. He argues that modern childhood is increasingly being defined by changes in the division of tasks and responsibilities between families, institutions and the government and the search for new balances in self-control and external control. As young children's dependency on intimate educators like their parents decreases, their dependency on a range of professional, formal educators increases, and these shifts run parallel to changes in their character formation and affect management. Whilst external compulsion by parents has become less dominant, there is now more social pressure for young children to conform to social expectations and control their own behaviour. In the daily interactions between young children and their parents, a search for balances between different forms of control is observable.

Castrén and Ketokivi (2015) illustrate the way that Elias's relational thinking can be used to illuminate these contradictory tendencies in lived family relationships. Elias's concept of interdependence can offer insightful ways to tease out the personally significant relations in which the meanings of family are anchored. They draw on a previous Finnish study on reconfigurations of family and kin relationships after separation or divorce (Castrén, 2008; Castrén and Maillochon, 2009). Family dissolution generates change and tension in a large number of relations and their study focused on the kin group composition after separation, especially on in-law relationships. Re-partnering generates even more turmoil, as questions arise about who will be included and excluded from the stepfamily's circle of significant relatives. In their study, figurations consisted of all the people that the research participants – 19 mothers and 15 fathers – considered as close or otherwise important and present in their lives.

Their analysis was conducted as a dialogical process between interviews on significant relationships, questionnaire data on these relationships and information on the figurational structure. In the narratives children were often mentioned as the reason to continue the relationship with former in-laws – the majority of participants not only had former in-laws in their figurations, typically children's biological relatives, but their relationship with former in-laws pointed to a stable 'enclave' of relations which were maintained during holidays, family rituals and celebrations, especially on children's birthdays.

Even though the narratives focused on current partnership as the main constituent of family groups, participants' relationships with their children from previous unions, with former partners and in-laws – all interconnected – formed a relational structure that constrained inclusion in or exclusion from the kin group. Moreover, the analysis of questionnaires showed how former in-laws were sometimes considered emotionally closer than present in-laws. This aspect was not displayed in the interviews at all. The structural position of the former in-laws in the kin group appeared to be quite stable in spite of separation, indicating that the figurations had not gone through an important transformation. Castrén and Ketokivi's study can therefore help to illuminate the multifaceted and complex dynamics in family relationships: despite structural and emotional pressure ('for the children's sake') towards maintaining contact, there is a tendency to downplay the role of former in-laws as personally significant.

Although it is clear that problems arise for young children during these family changes, the emphasis in past research has been on *adults'* accounts of their difficulties and responses to family transitions. The importance of understanding the perspectives of young children about their family situations is increasingly stressed by policy makers and those concerned with care and custody arrangements, yet there are still relatively few studies which have asked the views of young children. However, one important study by Dunn and Deater-Deckard (2001) asked children between four and seven years old to draw pictures of their families, examining who was included and excluded from their pictures. Each child was given a blank sheet of paper titled 'me and my family' and asked to draw a picture of their family. No further instructions were given and it was left up to the child to decide who she or he chose to include.

They concluded that the interviews, drawings and maps of their families revealed a notable sensitivity to the distinction between relationships with their birth parents and step-parents; young children with both step-parents and birth parents resident in the home were more likely to exclude their step-parents than their birth parents. For example, one child drew her mother, herself, her full sibling and half sibling, but left out her stepfather, her non-resident birth father and his current partner.

In the next section I will discuss the Romantic view of childhood and how it continues to exert such a strong influence on parental advice on the best way to bring up young children.

Romantic Concepts of Childhood

The eighteenth-century French philosopher Jean-Jacques Rousseau is an important figure for understanding the historical roots of Romantic childhood. Rousseau's utopian view of 'Nature' and childhood are conflated in *Emile* (1762), his famous fictionalised philosophical treatise about the ideal natural education of a young boy in the countryside. Rousseau (1991 [1762]) compares childhood with external and internal forms of nature, referring to nature as 'primitive dispositions'. He argues that nature is a *quality* in the young child, and warns that if this natural quality is not properly nurtured it will decay. As innocents, young children should be left to respond to nature and be protected from the risks and prejudices of social institutions.

Emile, his ideal boy, was not to learn to read until after he was 12: he must be free to roam outdoors in loose clothing, learning by his own interests and experience in a natural environment. Only in adolescence would Emile be allowed to learn to read and write and to master a craft. When he spoke of the corruption of natural childhood, Rousseau was referring to the vulnerability of young children to the vices of European adult society, which he clearly held in contempt as unnatural and contaminating. 'Everything is good as it comes from the hands of the Author of things; everything degenerates in the hands of man' (Rousseau, 1991 [1762]: 37).

This concept of 'nature' in Rousseau's *Emile* is based on a theory of *two worlds* that have to be strictly separated: one childish, isolated and innocent; the other adult, social and corrupt. The rebirth of society out of the education of nature would be the harmonising of these two worlds. In *Emile*, natural education is specifically designed to order a man's desires and capacities so that he desires only things that he can achieve by using his full capacities. It is a kind of recovery of the natural harmony between man's desires (passions) and his capacities (strength and reason) to fulfil those desires so that natural goodness can be maintained. This idea of natural goodness is most clearly manifested in Rousseau's concept of a primordial *amour de soi* (often translated as love of self), a natural inborn passion which directs man to self-preservation and happiness.

According to Rousseau, man's only natural passion is *amour de soi* and the others are modifications of it. When he criticises modern society, he mentions man's other basic passion, *amour-propre*, which is an extended form of *amour de soi* that represents man's need to enter into social relations: 'But *amour-propre*, which makes comparisons, is never content and never could be, because this sentiment, preferring ourselves to others, also demands others to prefer us to themselves, which is impossible' (Rousseau, 1991 [1762]: 213–214). In French moral literature in the seventeenth and early eighteenth centuries, writers such as François La Rochefoucauld and Blaise Pascal considered *amour de soi* as a negative force that must be restricted by education. The aim of education was not only growth but protection of the inner-self by living within the 'true' proportions of one's needs.

However, the dissemination of Rousseau's fame and ideas can also be explained by the highly detailed rules that regulated the lives of people in his society. We can interpret his natural child of innocence as a response to the advancing urban development of French society – the idealisation of nature was used by members of court-aristocratic circles as a counterpoint to the constraints of royal rule and suppression of feeling in court life (Elias, 2006). As more and more people moved into cities and towns, the young child became a symbol that was used to represent innocence and the 'Nature' that had been lost in adults' estrangement from the countryside. Elias (2009: 61) argues that the positive feelings surrounding the use of the word 'nature' make human beings 'behave as if they never could rely on regulations and compulsions they themselves impose on one another'.

To understand the significance of this statement we can turn to several places where Elias directly refers to Rousseau; in *The Court Society* (2006) he argues that to understand the influence of Rousseau within good court society (the *monde*), we need to explain the emancipation of feelings from the pressures of court rationality. Attempts to emancipate 'feeling' are 'always at the same time attempts to emancipate the individual from social pressure' (Elias, 2006: 122–123). Elias's interpretation can be used to explain why Rousseau was so keen to advocate a 'natural' education for the young Emile, one that ensured that he was divorced from the intricate webs of social relationships. Emile, the paradigmatic child of nature's education, was from his earliest days exercised in *self-sufficiency*. He is independent from others and can learn what is immediately around him without being disturbed. His uncovering of the romantic feelings associated with the use of the word 'nature' can alert us to the way that human beings, in different types of societies, attempt to disguise the strong levels of social support that they need from their relationships with one another. The meaning and resonance of Rousseau's advocacy of 'natural education' can therefore be viewed as a romantic dream about childhood, proposed by an adult philosopher keen to escape the social constraints of his society.

The important part played by the concept of 'Nature' in Rousseau's thought is often seen as a precursor to the more radical Romanticism of the late eighteenth century. The early Romantics – Blake, Wordsworth and Goethe – drew attention to the ideal of childhood as an unmediated source of experience within each individual. Their idea of an interior self with a personal history suggested that we all retain an aspect of our individual pasts in our 'psyches'. For Wordsworth, innocence was deeply rooted in the 'natural' world: the child is a part of his own childhood as remembered by an adult looking back in time. Central to this concept of the child is a sense of oneness between his body and the world that surrounded him in childhood.

According to Gittins (1998) this was the beginning of an important trend towards interiorisation, in which adults were more and more looking inwards, as well as backwards in time, to their own personal childhood. Steedman (1995) has traced this concept of 'interiority of the child' in the nineteenth century. She examines the various representations of Mignon, the homeless orphan (originally portrayed by Goethe (2013), the great German writer, in *Wilhelm Meister*) who was uprooted by adults training her to be an acrobat. Throughout the nineteenth century, this mythical image was a crucial source for intensive adult longing and desire – images of the remembered and imagined child were often woven together. And this Romantic image of the child continues until contemporary times. In a letter to one of his friends, Andrzej Plesniewicz, the great twentieth-century Polish writer Bruno Schulz revealed his Romantic project of restoring the lost unity of man, divinity and nature through the creative act of imagination:

> If it were possible to reverse development, to grasp some road back around to childhood again, to have its abundance and limitlessness once more – then that 'age of genius,' those 'messianic times' promised and sworn to us by all mythologies, would come to pass. My ideal goal is to 'mature' into childhood. That would be genuine maturity. (Schulz, 1989: 424, in Oklot, 2007: 135)

According to Oklot (2007), the 'maturing into childhood' contains Schulz's entire programme for literature, its epistemological and aesthetic foundations. It is not, however, a glorification of the naive creative spontaneity of a child. In Schulz, the artist has to regress and, at the same time, mature into childhood – to regain the young child's perspective without losing the present experience and direct him to the quest of finding the messianic time, which is always in the future. The image of a child allows him to reach the mythical origins, and the figure of an adult provides a language that can transform these immature epiphanies into poetic images.

As young children were increasingly being seen by adults as closer to 'nature', they needed to be protected from the more extreme forms of child labour, such as chimney-sweeping and prostitution. Working-class families were criticised by the Evangelicals in terms of the 'order of nature': 'In the order of nature, parents, and particularly fathers, would labour for the support of their young children' (Cunningham, 1991: 83). The distinctive 'nature' of childhood meant that young children were different from adults – child labour in factories was distorting the order of both 'nature' and England. Because young children were considered to be innately innocent, special and vulnerable, it was felt that they should be sheltered from the adult world. Adults therefore campaigned for state legislation that would give children protection.

One important social campaigner was Henry Mayhew, who, in December 1850, visited the greengrocers' markets of London as part of his Morning Chronicle series on *London Labour and the London Poor* (first published 1861). During this month, he met and interviewed the Little Watercress Girl, an eight-year-old who defined herself as a worker. She told Mayhew of her life at home with her mother, her brother and two sisters, and her mother's common-law husband, a scissor-grinder by trade. When Mayhew described her narrative, he placed it within a framework of anonymity and ignorance, yet he took from her a detailed account of family organisation, both at the economic and domestic levels. However, his attempt to present young children as utterly and incredibly strange, remote, filthy and products of impoverished home circumstances produced quite different evidence. Mayhew's concept of the 'lost' child distorted his interpretation to such an extent that he underestimated his subject's ability to explain in her own words her social and economic conditions.

Religious and Medical Moralities

In marked contrast to the natural goodness of the 'Romantic child' were the traditional beliefs held by members of the Evangelical Movement.

Despite their relatively small number, they were very influential through their prolific writings about childrearing practices. Their beliefs dominated both the advisory literature available to parents and children's own reading for nearly two centuries (Newson and Newson, 1974). During the eighteenth and nineteenth centuries, a severe view of childhood emerges, one where socialisation is seen as a battleground where the wills of stubborn children have to be broken, but for their own good. For the Evangelicals, the prospect of heaven and the threat of hell were major sources of motivation in their attempts to 'form the minds' of their own children. Each child enters the world as a wilful material force, is impish and harbours a potential for evil that can be mobilised if adults allow them to stray from the righteous path that God has provided.

In proclaiming 'Break the will, if you would not damn the child' Wesley (1872: 320) expressed the ever-present fear of damnation, in an age when most families would have lost at least one child. James Janeway, a Puritan minister, famous for his influential *A Token for Children* (1830), first published in 1672 and reprinted well into the middle of the nineteenth century, makes the connection between dying and hell quite explicit (see the Discussion Activity at the end of this chapter). From Janeway onwards, the pious and happy deaths of good little boys and girls are compared with the terrible deaths of irreligious children who were assumed to have passed straight to the eternal fires of hell. Young children's deaths are continuously described and lingered over in children's books of the eighteenth and nineteenth centuries. For example, the *Child's Companion* of 1829, a well-illustrated little volume of poems and stories, contains 13 deathbed scenes, together with one discourse on death and two poems inspired by gazing on children's graves. In a society in which death is such a familiar occurrence and an authoritarian God has unlimited powers to decide who will be rewarded through heaven or punished in hell, young children need to be prepared as carefully for death as for life. In the painting 'Childhood' (1896) by Charles Sims, a group of angelic children dressed in flowing white are acting out the funeral of a doll.

Miller (1987) sees strict aphorisms on childrearing such as 'spare the rod and spoil the child' or 'you have to be cruel to be kind' as part of a wider discourse on *poisonous pedagogy*. Poisonous pedagogy is the process by which adults rationalise their own needs and re-enact the humiliation they experienced in their own childhoods. This rationalisation disguises their own negative feelings and experiences, becoming part of a set of common-sense beliefs about what is good for young children and informing the larger debate on childcare and education. Phillips (2006: 106) points to the way that childhood can easily become the touchstone for how adults view themselves: their obsession with child development and with 'parenting skills' has burdened young children with the fears they harbour for their own sanity.

An evangelical concern to eradicate fears about 'the devil in the child' had important links with the medical-hygienist movement which dominated the 1920s and 1930s in Britain (Newson and Newson, 1974). Scientific mothercraft offered parents the hope that babies could be successfully reared provided that medical advice was faithfully followed: the vengeful God of heaven and hell was replaced by science, an equally authoritarian expert. A good example of this authoritarian advice was *The Mothercraft Manual* written by Liddiard (1928). Although this was not a government publication, it was extremely important before the Second World War, and even more significantly became the main vehicle for the principles of Sir Truby King (1937) and his Mothercraft Training Society. Babies needed to conform to adult expectations – in a sense, their wishes were suspect because they could conceal dangerous impulses or a rebellious determination to dominate the mother. Truby King (1937) believed that when mothers were in constant control, a 'good' baby was reared:

> The mother who 'can't be so cruel' as to wake her sleeping baby if he happens to be asleep at the appointed feeding-time, fails to realise that a few such wakings would be all she would have to resort to ... The establishment of perfect regularity of habits, initiated by 'feeding and sleeping by the clock', is the ultimate foundation of all-round obedience. (In Newson and Newson, 1974: 60–61)

'Natural' Development

During the inter-war years, a major shift in child management was developed under the influence of psychoanalysts like Susan Isaacs. Isaacs wanted parents and teachers to examine their *own* behaviours that might unwittingly increase any difficulties being experienced by the young child. Her main concern was to make people think about 'the various ways in which we can best foster [a child's] mental health' (Isaacs, 2006 [1937]: 134). In her book *The Nursery Years* (1932) she advised parents to observe young children in 'natural' play as an important part of their development, recommending that mothers take a more tolerant attitude towards prohibited practices like thumb-sucking and masturbation. All practitioners should use observational methods and collect systematic data that would enable educators to escape 'the narrow circle of our own experience' (Isaacs, 2006 [1937]: 135): by observing the 'deeper meaning of play' over an extended period of time, adults could become better pedagogues.

This growing awareness of parents towards their own behaviour was also reflected in the parenting literature produced in Australia during the inter-war years (Kitchens, 2007). Kitchens (2007) explores how authors of this literature placed limits on the use of violence, discouraging authoritarian disciplinary methods and promoting young children's independence and autonomy. She argues that these attempts to transform childrearing practices can be interpreted as part of a civilising process by which a greater capacity for self-control is expected from both young children and parents, revealing a gradual movement away from the use of emotional and physical violence.

A related and important theme that Kitchens (2007) identifies in the parenting literature is the issue of authority and control, or what Elias (2008) referred to as a loosening of the hierarchical structure of the parent–child relationship. Parents are encouraged to allow young children a degree of autonomy and to tolerate and respond to their developmental needs. This restructuring of the authority relationship has important implications not only for young children but for parents – accommodating to the 'natural' laws of child development is no easy task since it requires that both sides exercise continual restraint and self-control. Parents are encouraged to suppress feelings of anger and aggression when dealing with young children, even when their actions may bring about irritation and annoyance. The advice given to parents changed from the strictly authoritarian to the friendly, more persuasive approach: whereas in the 1930s, mothers were given solemn warnings about what would happen to them if they failed to enforce the rules, they are now given continual reassurances about what might possibly result from some mistaken actions.

By the 1940s and 1950s the influence of psychoanalytic theories, especially the work of Donald Winnicott and John Bowlby, was changing the advice given to parents. This was now more closely focused on the nature of the relationship between the mother and young child and their need for close contact (the strengths and limitations of attachment theory were previously discussed in Chapter 3). Benjamin Spock's *Common Sense Book of Baby and Child Care* (1946: 4) is the supreme example of the friendly, conversational approach that was given to parents – paternalistic enough to give confidence and reassurance, but willing to speak to the mother on equal terms: 'every baby needs to be smiled at, talked to, played with, fondled gently and lovingly … Be natural and comfortable and enjoy your baby'.

In a similar vein, the publication of Margaret Ribble's very influential book *The Rights of Infants* (1943) represented a humanitarian response to earlier and harsher infant-feeding regimes. There was a growing acceptance that babies' desires were legitimate, they needed not only their mothers' presence, but also the rocking, cuddling and lap play that had previously been forbidden. Newson and Newson (1974: 66) refer to this new trend as 'fun morality', in which the fundamental need of parents is to be happy in parenthood. To deprive babies of the 'natural' expression of maternal warmth would prevent the development of their social relationships and personalities.

'Designed by Nature, Made by Mum'

An important aspect of this 'maternal warmth' is the 'natural' woman who mothers and breastfeeds her infant. There is 'no single commitment as enduring, time-consuming, and emotionally compelling – as close to seeming necessary and natural – as the relation of a woman to her infant child' (Rosaldo, 2006: 24). In contemporary breastfeeding discourse, cultural constructions of 'nature' and the 'natural' represent such a positive force that it has become a term that has 'acquired the connotation of being inherently good, even moral' (Eyer, 1994: 78). The moral authority of nature has become so intensified in recent decades that nature has become positioned and understood as a sacred entity, supported by the growth of respect and 'popular reverence for nature and natural experiences' (Wall, 2001: 596). Yet this contributes to the confusion and disempowerment of mothers who encounter breastfeeding problems (Van Esterik, 1989). One of the contradictions in the current breastfeeding discourse is that Western women live in societies where breastfeeding has lapsed to such an extent that it now needs to be retaught through scientific and professional advice.

Breastfeeding literature sets great store on the 'naturalness' of breastfeeding, and campaigns have been quick to emphasise the naturalness of breast milk. The British National Health Service (NHS) advises women that 'breast milk is the only natural food designed for your baby'; an NHS-endorsed booklet (National Health Service, 2014) carries the slogan 'Designed by Nature, Made by Mum'. The philosophy of mothering advocated by organisations such as La Leche League emphasises the importance of an intimate, physical relationship between mother and baby, 'naturally' fulfilled through breastfeeding. However the literature that emphasises the naturalness, purity and simplicity of breastfeeding, couching it in a language of ease and convenience such as 'It's free', 'It's available whenever and wherever your baby needs a feed' also distorts female expectations of breastfeeding.

By lending itself to the view that all women can breastfeed successfully, portraying potential issues as surmountable, this literature trivialises the real problems women face as well as the diversity of women's embodied experience. A study of 25 Australian mothers' breastfeeding experiences reports that they recognised that mothering and breastfeeding centred on a private world but yearned to be part of public life again (Schmied and Lupton, 2001). Women were exhorted to follow their nature, which increasingly confined them to the private, domestic sphere. They were considered to be less able than men to transcend their nature and take part in the cultural activities that are firmly part of the male world (Ortner, 2006). As a 'natural' phenomenon, breastfeeding belonged to the area still regarded as the mother's concern, unlike the management of childbirth which became controlled by the male dominated medical world (Maher, 1995).

Parker (2015) argues that although this socially constructed infant-feeding discourse is very persuasive, it can be disempowering for women, limiting their presence in public life, devaluing their work and presenting beliefs as scientific 'facts'. It is frequently invoked today to serve certain groups' distinct purposes to be true to 'nature', deployed in multiple ways to shape women's choices and activities. Choosing to breastfeed may be instinctive to many women, one mother said 'It's obviously natural with immunity things and everything else, and … that's the way nature intended' (Dykes, 2005: 2286). But for some women their experiences are clearly not 'instinctive' because breastfeeding has not been the ubiquitously 'natural' state of affairs in European countries for many centuries.

Conclusions

This chapter has focused on the major transformations in contemporary family relationships and parenting since the mid-twentieth century, discussing the shifting balances of power between men, women and young children. The pace and complexity of this dynamic change in family relations, whether within a marriage, relationship or post-separation, places demands on people to adjust to this change, removing the support of existing social forms: young children and parents 'are compelled to a greater degree than before to work out a modus vivendi with each other through their own efforts, that is, more purposively' (Elias, 2008: 40). Elias points out that it is precisely the concept of 'the family' as a 'natural' social institution which makes this process more difficult, because it generates disappointment and frustration that reality does not live up to the ideal. He argues that we need to acknowledge that the task constituted by the formation, establishment and continuation of intimate relationships within these contradictory social processes is one that is more effectively tackled consciously and deliberately.

I focused on the different advice that parents are given by discussing some of the major shifts that have occurred, from a more authoritarian view of parenting which concentrates on the needs of parents to control their offspring, to a more relaxed view where scientific theories advocated the importance of responding to young children's requirements, to today, where there has been a gradual erosion of power imbalances in relationships between parents and young children. According to Elias (2008), these changes can be explained by a process of informalisation, a period of movement from an authoritarian to a more egalitarian parent–child relationship where there is a loosening of barriers of authority in relations between young children and adults.

I argued that an important way of understanding these processes is to examine the emergence and development of the key concept of 'nature' which has been used to inform and shape changing historical beliefs about the best way for parents to bring up young children. Some of the most influential patterns of parental advice that have evolved since the eighteenth century can be traced to the Romantic vision of the child as 'natural', 'pure' and 'innocent'. According to Plotz (2001: 24), the young child imagined by the Romantics represented a lost childhood 'immune to the pressures of history': isolated and solitary, imaginative and creative, but close to nature and possessing erotic and emotional authority. The 'innocent' child that needed protection from the corruption of adult society was developed by philosophers such as Rousseau to uncover the deeper, more intuitive parts of ourselves concealed under the armour of adulthood. The 'inner child' remains within adulthood and is reinterpreted within an idealised process – a remembered child full of feeling and joyousness. From the seventeenth century, this Romantic image became a crucial source for intensive adult longing and desire.

However, Davis (2011) has offered an important reappraisal of the concept of childhood innocence as a way of testing some of the dominant constructions of childhood. He argues that any insistence on a high Romantic turning point in the fortunes of childhood innocence oversimplifies the past: contrary to the findings of Ariès, he argues that the lost histories of innocence are more diverse and complex than established conventions suggest. In the next chapter we will examine how this dominant theme about protecting the innocence of young children informs contemporary debates about the pervasive influence of television and new media technologies.

DISCUSSION ACTIVITY

Read below the advisory literature available to parents in the early nineteenth century and discuss the following questions:

Are you willing to go to hell, to be burned with the devil and his angels? ... O! Hell is a terrible place ... Did you ever hear of a little child that died ... and if other children die, why you may be sick and die? ... How do you know but that you may be the next child that may die? ... Now tell me, my pretty dear child, what will you do? (James Janeway, *A Token for Children* (1830), quoted in Newson and Newson, 1974: 57)

1. How would parents in the past make sure that their children were good and did not go to hell?

2. What kind of images of young children does the television programme *Supernanny* draw upon and how does it do this?

3. Identify some of the modern-day parenting manuals which are available for mothers and fathers? In what way is their advice different from the past?

Further Reading

Ellie Lee, Charlotte Faircloth, Jan Macvarish and Jennie Bristow (2014) *Parenting Culture Studies.* Basingstoke: Palgrave Macmillan.

A provocative book by academics at the University of Kent that further develops the critique of parenting first offered by Frank Furedi, warning that expert intervention into childrearing might not empower parents, but rather undermine them. The authors examine why bringing up children has grown from a private family matter to a huge 'parenting' industry supported by various experts and policy makers. Key chapters cover the 'intensification of parenting', the rise of the 'parenting expert', the politicising of parent-child relationships and the weakening of bonds between generations.

Julia Brannen (2004) 'Childhoods across the Generations: Stories from Women in Four-Generation English Families', *Childhood*, 11(4): 409-428.

There has been little systematic research in Britain focusing upon people's accounts of their childhoods across family generations. In this article Brannen explores the meanings of childhood for women who were born in three distinctive historical periods. The oldest generation, the great-grandmothers born around the First World War (1911-21), dwelt on the importance of families being able to provide children with materially secure childhoods and family lives, while the middle generation, grandmothers born around the Second World War (1940–48), stressed the importance of parents providing psychological security for the individual child. The youngest generation, mothers born in the late 1960s to early 1970s (1965–75), emphasised their own agency in shaping their children's childhoods. All three generations referred to the importance of grandmothers in children's childhoods, especially in working-class families. In periods in which mothers worked when they were 'supposed' to be at home, grandmothers were seen as parental figures as well as carers.

Joanne Bailey (2014) 'The History of Mum and Dad: Recent Historical Research on Parenting in England from the 16th to 20th Centuries', *History Compass*, 12(6): 489–507.

Bailey provides a good overview of some of the recent historical scholarship on how parenting has changed over time. She reviews this scholarship by identifying four significant arguments: first, the shifting gender constructions that have reshaped expectations about mothers' and fathers' roles. Although paternal breadwinning and maternal care have always been important, at times fathers have been commended for caring for infants and mothers for economic provision in terms of their offspring. Secondly, the material aspects of life have influenced different forms of parental expression and practice. Until relatively recently, parents struggled against high rates of infant and child mortality: nursing children, preparing them for death and the afterlife and coping with grief. Thirdly, levels of wealth and social class affect parenting, with working-class, poor and lone parents especially vulnerable to family disruption due to poverty, ill-health and unemployment. Fourthly, the parameters of 'bad' or deviant parenting have shifted over time. This kind of labelling offers numerous insights for understanding parenting in its wider social, economic and cultural contexts.

References

Beck, U. (1992) *Risk Society: Towards a New Modernity*. London: Sage.

Beck, U. and Beck-Gernsheim, E. (2002) *Individualization: Institutionalized Individualism and its Social and Political Consequences*. London: Sage.

Blair, T. (1998) *The Third Way: New Politics for the New Century*. London: Fabian Society.

Castrén, A.M. (2008) 'Post-Divorce Family Configurations', in E. Widmer and R. Jallinoja (eds), *Beyond the Nuclear Family: Families in a Configurational Perspective*. Bern: Peter Lang, pp. 233–254.

Castrén, A.M. and Ketokivi, K. (2015) 'Studying the Complex Dynamics of Family Relationships: A Figurational Approach', *Sociological Research Online*, 20(1): 3. Available at: www.socresonline.org.uk/20/1/3.html

Castrén, A.M. and Maillochon, F. (2009) 'Who Chooses the Wedding Guests, the Couple or the Family? Individual Preferences and Relational Constraints in France and Finland', *European Societies*, 11(3): 369–389.

The Child's Companion (1829) London: The Religious Tract Society.

Churchill, H. (2011) *Parental Rights and Responsibilities: Analysing Social Policy and Lived Experiences*. Bristol: Policy Press.

Cunningham, H. (1991) *The Children of the Poor: Representations of Childhood since the Seventeenth Century*. Oxford: Blackwell.

Davis, R.A. (2011) 'Brilliance of a Fire: Innocence, Experience and the Theory of Childhood', *Journal of Philosophy of Education*, 45(2): 379–397.

Dunn, J. and Deater-Deckard, K. (2001) *Children's Views of their Changing Families*. York: Joseph Rowntree Foundation.

Dykes, F. (2005) '"Supply" and "Demand": Breastfeeding as Labour', *Social Science and Medicine*, 60(10): 2283–2293.

Edwards, R. and Gillies, V. (2012) 'Farewell to Family? Notes on an Argument for Retaining the Concept', *Families, Relationships and Societies*, 1(1): 63–69.

Elias, N. (2006) *The Court Society*. Dublin: UCD Press [Collected Works, vol. 2].

Elias, N. (2008) 'The Civilising of Parents', in *Essays II: On Civilising Processes, State Formation and National Identity*. Dublin: UCD Press [Collected Works, vol. 15], pp. 14–40.

Elias, N. (2009) 'On Nature', in *Essays I: On the Sociology of Knowledge and the Sciences*. Dublin: UCD Press [Collected Works, vol. 14], pp. 53–65.

Eyer, D.E. (1994) 'Mother-Infant Bonding: A Scientific Fiction', *Human Nature*, 5(1): 69–94.

Furedi, F. (2008) *Paranoid Parenting: Why Ignoring the Experts May be Best for Your Child*. London/New York: Continuum.

Gabb, J. and Silva, E. (2011) 'Introduction to Critical Concepts: Families, Intimacies and Personal Life', *Sociological Research Online*, 16(4). Available at: www.socresonline.org.uk/16/4/23.html

Gillies, V. (2008) 'Childrearing, Class and the New Politics of Parenting', *Sociology Compass*, 2(3): 1079–1095.

Gillies, V. (2011) 'From Function to Competence: Engaging with the New Politics of Family', *Sociological Research Online*, 16(4). Available at: www.socresonline.org.uk/16/4/11.html

Gittins, D. (1998) *The Child in Question*. London: Macmillan.

Goethe, J.W. (2013) *Wilhelm Meister*. Richmond: Alma Classics.

Hardyment, C. (2007) *Dream Babies, Childcare Advice from John Locke to Gina Ford*. London: Francis Lincoln.

Hollway, W. (2006) *The Capacity to Care: Gender and Ethical Subjectivity*. Abingdon: Routledge.

Isaacs, S. (1932) *The Nursery Years*. London: Routledge and Kegan Paul.

Isaacs, S. (2006 [1937]) 'The Educational Value of the Nursery School', in R. Parker-Rees and J. Willan (eds), *Vol. 1, Histories and Traditions, Early Years Education: Major Themes in Education*. Abingdon: Routledge, pp. 134–155.

Jamieson, L. (2011) 'Intimacy as a Concept: Explaining Social Change in the Context of Globalisation or Another Form of Ethnocentricism', *Sociological Research Online*, 16(4). Available at: www.socresonline.org.uk/16/4/15.html

Janeway, J. (1830) *A Token for Children*. London: Religious Tract Society.

Kitchens, R. (2007) 'The Informalization of the Parent-Child Relationship: An Investigation of Parent Discourses Produced in Australia in the Inter-War Years', *Journal of Family History*, 32(4): 459–478.

Liddiard, M. (1928) *The Mothercraft Manual*. London: Churchill.

Lister, R. (2006a) 'Children (but not Women) First: New Labour Child Welfare and Gender', *Critical Social Policy*, 26(2): 315–335.

Lister, R. (2006b) 'An Agenda for Children: Investing in the Future or Promoting Well-being in the Present?', in J. Lewis (ed.), *Children, Changing Families and Welfare States*. Cheltenham: Edward Elgar, pp. 51–68.

Maher, V. (1995) 'Breast-feeding and Maternal Depletion: Natural Law or Cultural Arrangements', in V. Maher (ed.), *The Anthropology of Breast-feeding: Natural Law or Social Construct*. Oxford: Berg, pp. 151–181.

Mayhew, H. (1861) *London Labour and the London Poor*. London: Griffin, Bohn & Company.

Miller, A. (1987) *Thou Shalt Not be Aware: Society's Betrayal of the Child*. London: Pluto.

Morgan, D. (2011) *Rethinking Family Practices*. Basingstoke/New York: Palgrave Macmillan.

National Health Service (2014) *Essential Guide to Feeding and Caring for your Baby*. Truro: NHS/Real Baby Milk.

Newson, J. and Newson, E. (1974) 'Cultural Aspects of Childrearing in the English-speaking World', in M.P.M. Richards (ed.), *The Integration of a Child into a Social World*. Cambridge: Cambridge University Press, pp. 53–82.

Oklot, M. (2007) 'Maturing into Childhood: An Interpretive Framework of a Modern Cosmogony and Poetics', *Journal of Comparative Poetics. Childhood: Creativity and Representation*, 27: 131–153.

Ortner, S.B. (2006) 'Is Female to Male as Nature is to Culture?', in M.Z. Rosaldo and L. Lamphere (eds) *Woman, Culture and Society*. Stanford: Stanford University Press, pp. 67–84.

Palmer, S. (2006) *Toxic Childhood: How the Modern World is Damaging Our Children and What We Can Do About It*. London: Orion.

Parker, L. (2015) 'Breastfeeding – a Window into Mothering Itself'. Masters thesis, Department of Anthropology, London School of Economics.

Parton, N. (2006) *Safeguarding Children: Early Intervention and Surveillance in a Late Modern Society*. Basingstoke: Palgrave.

Phillips, P. (2006) *Going Sane*. London: Penguin.

Plotz, J. (2001) *Romanticism and the Vocation of Childhood*. New York: Palgrave.

Plummer, K. (2003) *Intimate Citizenship: Private Decisions and Public Dialogues*. Seattle, WA: University of Washington Press.

Ramaekers, S. and Suissa, J. (2011) *The Claims of Parenting: Reasons, Responsibility and Society*. Dordrecht: Springer.

Ribbens McCarthy, J. (2012) 'The Powerful Relational Language of "Family": Togetherness, Belonging and Personhood', *The Sociological Review*, 60(1): 68–90.

Ribble, M. (1943) *The Rights of Infants*. New York: Columbia University Press.

Rodger, J.J. (2012) "Regulating the Poor": Observations on the "Structural Coupling" of Welfare, Criminal Justice and the Voluntary Sector in a "Big Society"', *Social Policy and Administration*, 46(4): 413–443.

Rosaldo, M.Z. (2006) 'Woman, Culture and Society: A Theoretical Overview', in M.Z. Rosaldo and L. Lamphere (eds), *Woman, Culture and Society*. Stanford: Stanford University Press, pp. 17–43.

Rousseau, J.J. (1991 [1762]) *Emile or On Education*. London: Penguin.

Schmied, V. and Lupton, D. (2001) 'Blurring the Boundaries: Breastfeeding and Maternal Subjectivity', *Sociology of Health and Illness*, 23(2): 234–250.

Schulz, B. (1989) *Opowiadania. Wybor esejow i listow*, ed. J. Jarzebski. Wroclaw: Ossolineum.

Smart, C. (2007) *Personal Life*. Cambridge: Polity.

Spock, B. (1946) *The Common Sense Book of Baby and Child Care*. New York: Duell, Sloan and Pearce.

Statham, J. and Smith, M. (2010) *Issues in Earlier Intervention: Identifying and Supporting Children with Additional Needs*. London: HMSO – Department of Children, Schools and Families.

Steedman, C. (1995) *Strange Dislocations: Childhood and the Idea of Human Interiority, 1780–1930*. Cambridge, MA: Harvard University Press.

Truby King, F. (1937) *Feeding and Care of Baby*, revised edition. London: Oxford University Press.

Van Daalen, R. (2010) 'Children and Childhood in Dutch Society and Dutch Sociology', *Current Sociology*, 58(2): 351–368.

Van Esterik, P. (1989) *Beyond the Breast–Bottle Controversy*. New Brunswick, NJ: Rutgers University Press.

Wall, G. (2001) 'Moral Constructions of Motherhood in Breastfeeding Discourse', *Gender and Society*, 15(4): 592–610.

Wesley, J. (1872) *Works*. London: Wesleyan Conference Office.

Young, M. and Wilmott, P. (1957) *Family and Kinship in East London*. Harmondsworth: Penguin.

7

NEW MEDIA TECHNOLOGIES AND THE SEXUALISATION OF CHILDHOOD

Introduction

This chapter focuses on the debate within contemporary childhood about the moral dangers that new media technologies pose for young children. I begin my discussion by looking at the controversies that surround the development of television and young children's access to electronic technologies, outlining Postman's (1994) influential claim that adults should try to protect them by keeping secrets about sexual behaviour. Authors like Palmer (2006) argue that young children's exposure to visual culture, commercialism and new technologies produces a toxic cocktail that is damaging to their social development, creating high levels of anxiety and contaminating their experience of childhood. In the UK regular surges of media-fuelled moral panics have focused on video nasties, computer games and concerns about Internet bullying in the digital age. We explore how the sociological concept of 'moral panic' is helpful because it can be used to explain the emergence of 'public' concerns about a particular social problem in early childhood, one that is likely to involve three distinctive discourses: a discourse about the specific threat, for example paedophilia; a moral panic discourse, which is perceived as a threat to the moral order; and a discourse about evil as beyond understanding (Astroff and Nyberg, 1992).

However, later in the chapter I shift my attention from speculation about the harms posed to young children by television and new media technologies to focus on some of the underlying images of childhood that drive the moral panic agenda. In recent years, the 'sexualisation of childhood' has moved into the centre ground of public policy and international debate. This contemporary issue has been identified as a major concern at national levels – for instance, the Australian Senate's 2007 inquiry (Australian Senate, 2008) that followed the controversy over a think-tank report entitled *Corporate Paedophilia* (Rush and la Nauze, 2006). In Britain, the New Labour government commissioned a report on sexualisation from the 'celebrity psychologist' Linda Papadopoulos (2010), while the previous coalition government appointed Reg Bailey, Chief Executive of the Christian pro-family charity the Mothers' Union, to review 'the sexualisation and commercialisation of childhood' (DfE, 2011).

I then discuss some of the major assumptions that lie behind the fears that adults have about young children's use of new technologies, discussing how childhood and sexuality share deep historical roots. The 'innocent child' of philosophical and social discourses from the eighteenth century onwards (see the discussion in the previous chapter) was galvanised in the same historical milieu as contemporary notions of sexuality (Egan and Hawkes, 2010). As Jackson (1982) has argued, childhood and sexuality share a similar conceptual history – sexuality and sexual knowledge are crucial dimensions in the contemporary Western definition of childhood and adulthood, maintaining boundaries between them.

But why is it so important for adults to protect children's innocence? The construction of childhood in Western societies within discourses of developmental psychology (see Chapter 3) strongly influences young children's precarious and difficult relationship to sexuality. Children's access to sexual knowledge before it is considered to be developmentally appropriate – usually defined within a moral framework – is perceived as corrupting their innocence, potentially leading to promiscuity and immature sexual activity. The availability of sexual information is hardly ever treated as a positive thing – the dark suspicion of a direct link between knowing about sex and doing sex has tended to focus attention on protection (Robinson, 2012). The 'knowing child', the young child who is perceived to 'know too much' about sexuality for his or her age is considered highly problematic for adults.

The Disappearance of Childhood

According to Postman (1994), childhood evolved between the sixteenth and eighteenth centuries because of the demands that adults made on children to read. It can be traced to the rise of print culture, particularly the book, which created a space between a literate adult world and children who needed access to a world of civilisation, culture and knowledge. Book learning is a key aspect of this process as it enables adults to control information that young children are not supposed to know about – language and cultural secrets had to be gradually revealed through the printed word, culminating in sexual enlightenment. This process became institutionalised through mass schooling, a system of learning organised around young children's age-related, incremental acquisition of knowledge.

Postman (1994) argued that childhood started disappearing in the second half of the twentieth century because the moral and cultural boundaries that separate young children and adults were gradually being eroded due to the influence of electronic media. The immediacy of television undercuts the adult-regulated process of reading and development, flattening the boundaries between adulthood and childhood. Shame becomes diluted and demystified as electronic media reveal the content of the adult world to young children by making sexual knowledge directly available to them (Postman, 1994: 85). They are therefore losing their innocence as they become more exposed to the same images, ideas and risks as their parents.

Postman refers to Elias' (2012) *On the Process of Civilisation* as a great book, using various aspects of its argument to support his major claim that shame is the defining feature of childhood, writing that 'without a well-developed idea of shame, childhood cannot exist' (Postman, 1994: 19). Elias's argument illustrates how a modern view of childhood develops as adults keep sexual secrets from young children: it uses Erasmus' *Colloquies* to illustrate the changing standards of shame since the Middle Ages, the importance of self-restraint over instinctual life and the separation between public and private life. A good summary of Postman's argument is contained in the following quotation:

> Children, in other words, are immersed in a world of secrets, surrounded by mystery and awe; a world that will be made intelligible to them by adults who will teach them, in stages, how shame is transformed into a set of moral directives. From the child's point of view, shame gives power and authority to adulthood. For adults know, *whereas children do not*, what

words are shameful to use, what subjects are shameful to discuss, what acts are deemed necessary to privatize. (Postman, 1994: 86, my emphasis)

Postman therefore believed that greater censorship and tighter control over the mass media was necessary so that sex and sexuality could be kept 'secret' from young children.

Sexuality and Moral Panics

Young children learn early that talking about sex and sexuality, especially with adults, is taboo. From an early age they are actively trying to make sense of and sort through the 'bits and pieces' of information they receive about sexuality (Davies and Robinson, 2010; Plummer, 1995). They engage in meaning-making around sexuality in their early lives, based on the limited information (stereotypes and myths) that they receive from families, peers, television, the Internet, and through observing others, especially older children, youth or adults. They often frame their understandings within other contexts, such as observing the sexual practices of family pets and animals, which is often used as a source for building knowledge about human experiences. A five-year-old child participating in Davies and Robinson's (2010: 257) research on children's sexual knowledge explained how she perceived becoming pregnant and having a baby: 'When the sperm meets the egg that turns it to an egg; the egg hatches and then the baby comes out.' Because young children's misinformation is frequently viewed as 'cute' and 'amusing' some adults choose not to intervene in correcting it (Robinson and Jones Diaz, 2006).

When the boundaries of what is perceived to be 'appropriate' knowledge for young children are transgressed, the concept of a moral panic is regularly mobilised in the popular media. A reoccurring theme of moral panics over the past 150 years has been the life of the child (Egan and Hawkes, 2010): accounts of young children in the media frequently begin by tracking back through history, from contemporary concerns about the Internet or video games to earlier fears about the influence of television and the cinema, through debates about music hall and popular literature in the nineteenth century. Even the ancient Greek philosopher Plato excluded the dramatic poets from his ideal Republic on the grounds that they had a harmful influence on the young (see Critcher, 2008; Davies, 2010). While each panic may appear specific, the recurrence of similar anxieties is seen to indicate a broader underlying continuity which is seen to recur, both across time and across different cultural contexts. According to Critcher (2008: 100), this kind of media panic has four key characteristics: a reworking of the theme of the innocent child corrupted by culture; the debate is actually about something else than it appears to be; campaigners often have ulterior motives; and it is always bound up with anxieties about the state of social order.

Each of these characteristics can be seen in the application of moral panic theory to debates about young children's media consumption. In such debates the perennial theme of the corruption of childhood innocence is continually reworked. Buckingham and Bragg (2004) have suggested such panics involve a form of displacement: they are about something other than they at first appear to be. Public campaigns against child pornography and young children's access to sexual knowledge are presented as evidence of a more general permissiveness exemplified by increased violence, drug use and criminal activity. The panic is not ultimately about young children or about the media at all: it is about much broader concerns regarding social change, such as a fear of technological and commercial innovation, or a fear of modernity. Buckingham and Bragg (2004: 15) argue that moral panics should be seen as imaginative projections that articulate anxieties about the fear of change and promote evocations of a better past, one where 'we are encouraged to look back to a golden age of innocence, well before the media led us all to "carnal hell"'.

What is therefore missing in theories of moral panic is a strong sense of the historical context in which such claims are made and why they are being made by those people in that way at that time (Buckingham and Jensen, 2012). Continuity is emphasised at the expense of change, and the past is judged from the perspective of the present, as though such concerns were merely timeless (Rohloff and Wright, 2010). These sensationalised stories can more fruitfully be explained as a deeply cyclical process that surrounds the mass media and its influence on the sexuality of young children. Historical narratives on the risks associated with dangerous novels in the 1890s, comic books in the 1950s, television in the 1980s and the Internet and growth of new media technologies in our contemporary culture share a common theme – fears about the corruption of childhood innocence and the need for protection.

Young Children's Access to Television

In the 1950s, young children's exposure to non-print media was limited to television, film and radio. Although it is not possible to identify the hours of television young children watched in this period, older people interviewed about their memories report that it was minimal, as they spent most of their leisure time playing outdoors (Marsh and Bishop, 2014). In the beginning of children's television, programming was influenced by a public service mission of entertainment, education and information, with a strong sense of moral constraint and responsibility. Young children's viewing should be guided and restricted: 'restraint in viewing will be encouraged in the interests of programme quality. ... it will need the co-operation of parents and consistency in planning over a period of time' (Adams, 1950: 86).

Children's television was to act as a moral and developmental guide, excluding the dangerous areas and signposting those that suited children best. Oswell (1995), for example, argues that a BBC programme series in the 1950s entitled, *Watch with Mother*, emerged out of a number of questions about the emotional well-being of the child in terms of the psychological dynamics of the family. In the planning stages of *Watch with Mother* there was clearly some reticence about the introduction of television for very young children and concern about its effects on the 'proper' mode of conduct within the home. An internal BBC memo is very revealing about the expected role of mothers in the household (6 March 1950):

> We had a special panel to advise us consisting of the repre-sentatives of the Ministry of Education, the Institute of Child Development, the Nursery Schools' Association, and some edu-cational child psychologists, and I think they would be pretty sure to squeak if you were to publicise any television programme for very young children as something that would set mother free to get about her other business, even though that might be in fact what happened. (Oswell, 1995: 37)

Continuity and scheduling were central to the guiding process, with the clearest signpost being the fundamental structure of the schedule. Under-fives were given their own separate afternoon slot. An hour of children's programmes was scheduled between 5 pm and 6 pm, to be followed immediately by a shutdown of an hour or more. The 'tod-dlers' truce' between 6 pm and 7 pm was what Owen Reed (Head of Children's Programmes) called an 'hour of protective silence', a period of non-transmission that served as a division between children's and adults' viewing. This blank zone was meant to insulate young children from the stories of 'rape', 'abortion' and 'capital punishment' which might be part of the news bulletin. The toddler's truce ended in 1957, mainly as a result of pressures from new commercial companies such as ITV, but the underlying principle of protecting children still remains, especially in the 9 o'clock watershed (Buckingham et al., 1999).The 9 o'clock watershed, gradually introduced in the early 1960s, was intended to provide a signal to parents that a point had been reached after which programmes may be unsuitable for family viewing.

The development of the children's watershed is a useful site to explore the way that adults try to protect young children by keeping secrets about sexual behaviour. I will outline some of the historical context that led to the development of the children's watershed on British television, before reviewing some of the recent policies developed by the Office for Communications (Ofcom) to regulate television programmes when young children are viewing. The British regulatory authority Ofcom applies the watershed to legitimise its decisions about explicit sexual images, attempting to impose a certain degree of control over what it considers to be harmful in the content of certain programmes. Their policies of regulation mirror important tensions about the best way to protect young children from adult programming and institutional conflict over the balance between government control and self-regulation by young children and parents.

The watershed seems to have emerged in a somewhat piecemeal fashion following the publication of the O'Conor Report in 1960 (BBC/ITA, 1960) which was not fixed until 1962. It placed its central emphasis on what it considered to be the most important fact to emerge from Himmelweit et al.'s (1958) influential collection of research studies – young children were watching substantial amounts of 'adult' programmes between 6 pm and 9 pm, yet programmes designed for them were reaching comparatively low audiences. Significantly, the Report noted the 'stigma apparently attached to programmes known by children to be intended for them' and commented that the BBC's audience share between 5 pm and 6 pm increased when the generic title 'Children's Television' was dropped.

The O'Conor Report became an important site of struggle over autonomy, control and self-regulation, highlighting one of the central dilemmas of broadcasting: how to acknowledge the presence of children without having to dilute programmes to make them suitable for a family audience, while also taking into consideration that 'programmes designed for the largest audience depend on material which is unsuitable for children' (BBC/ITA, 1960: 3).The broadcasters resisted government control by rejecting the O'Conor Committee's recommendation that educational advisors be involved in the production of children's programmes. Rather, they attempted to deflect public concern by producing internal codes of practice, which to a large extent became their favoured response in the following decades. The BBC and ITA's joint reference to the Report stated firmly that they 'do not believe that the needs of children should be allowed to determine the nature of television output up to 9.00 p.m.' (BBC/ITA, 1960: 2). Tensions can also be seen in the argument that was made by the Independent Television Companies' Association that parents should be responsible for their children's viewing and for ensuring that they are 'critical and selective'. But this was strongly rejected in the text of the Report.

Buckingham et al. (1999: 152) have therefore argued that 'at the heart of many debates about television is the child who needs protection': not only has 'protectionism' been an ongoing important part of scheduling, but it is also used to justify regulatory approaches to television. The Pilkington Report of 1962, for example, criticised ITV for its reliance on entertainment genres such as Westerns and called for changes in ITV programming policy, partly on the grounds that it was having adverse effects on children, 'who are normally protected from outside influences and therefore especially vulnerable' (Pilkington Committee, 1962: 5).

Regulation and New Media Consumption

In the UK the Communications Act (2003) required that the regulator (Ofcom) drew up a code for television and radio, setting standards for programmes on matters such as protecting the under-18s, harm and offence, sponsorship, fairness and privacy. A key change in the Act was the standards objective which requires that members of the public have 'adequate protection' from 'offensive and harmful material'. This was an important departure from the notion of 'good taste and decency', which had been applied in the Broadcasting Act (1990) to regulate the depiction of violence, especially 'when large numbers of children and young persons may be expected to be watching the programmes'.

Since the regulatory authority Ofcom was set up in 2003, it has regularly undertaken research among parents about the level of concerns related to the type of content that children watch on television and also measures parents' views about the time of the watershed and whose responsibility it is to protect children. It has a statutory duty to ensure that under-18s are protected. This is one of the most fundamental aspects of the Code and for Ofcom's regulation of standards in broadcasting. The emphasis on protection is very evident under the *Ofcom Broadcasting Code* (2015), where Section One is entitled, 'Protecting the Under 18s'. A fundamental requirement underpinning the rules in Section One of the Code is the application of the watershed, which applies to television only. The watershed starts at 9 pm, and material unsuitable for children should not, in general, be shown between 9 pm and 5.30 am. In Rule 1.4 in Ofcom's *Guidance Notes* (2015), it states that 'the watershed plays a crucial role for parents and carers with children aged 5 to 8 and trust in pre-watershed programming is essential, particularly leading up to 19.30'.

However, concerns about regulation and media consumption by young children have significantly changed over time due to the growth of the Internet and mobile technologies. In a similar way to the controversial debate about Postman's (1994) argument about the 'disappearance' of childhood, new media technologies and their content have eroded the notion of an age-related and gradual acquisition of sexual knowledge by young children. In contemporary society, young children grow up immersed in popular culture – parents and family members buy toys, books and games linked to television and film characters – and as they age, they develop their own media interests and passions (Marsh et al., 2005). Despite more and more children of primary-school age gaining access to the Internet, most of the research still concerns teenagers, with only 6% of studies including children aged five or younger (Ólafsson et al., 2013). The EU Kids Online study by Livingstone et al. (2011) found that children aged 15-16 years started using the Internet when they were 11 years old, while the 9–10-year-old children said that they were around seven years old when they started to use it.

As UK homes acquire more digital technologies that are more portable and diverse, younger children are using the Internet at home and at school. In the UK, Ofcom (2014) reported that screen use for 3–4-year-olds is 14 hours of television, 6.6 hours on the Internet and 6.1 hours gaming per week. The Ofcom survey (2015) found that the tablet is the one media device that has grown most in popularity amongst 5–7-year-olds in recent years, with 69% using it in 2015 as compared to 54% in 2014. Over half of 3–4-year-olds (51%) and 5–7-year-olds (49%) now use their tablet to go online (Ofcom, 2015), and its most common use is playing games, primarily for entertainment rather than for educational purposes. Not surprisingly, parents indicate that their children's favourite websites are CBeebies, YouTube and Disney, with YouTube growing the most in popularity (Childwise, 2014).

Although this data is a very useful starting point, we still know very little about how apps are used by young children. There have been repeated calls regarding the urgent need for research into the media and technology use of this age group (Buckingham, 2005; Holloway et al., 2013). This gap in knowledge is of particular concern given that apps are a large and growing market: Shuler reported in 2012 that 72% of the top-selling apps in the education section of Apple's app store were aimed at the pre-school age group. Such an under-researched area requires studies that can explain how young children use tablets and the types of apps with which they engage.

A recent study by Marsh et al. (2015) begins to offer some insight into the use of tablets by young children. This study had four separate but overlapping phases. First they conducted an online survey of 2,000 parents or caregivers of 0–5-year-olds in the UK, which was then followed by in-depth case studies of pre-school children's use of tablet apps in six families. Phase 3 consisted of observations of and interviews with children in Foundation Stages 1 and 2 using tablet apps, including augmented reality apps, with Phase 4 analysing the 10 apps used in Phase 3 in order to identify their affordances for the promotion of play and creativity. The results indicated that in households that own tablets, young children have extensive access to them – 25% of under threes and 37% of 3–5-year-olds own their own tablets. Others share their use with parents, siblings and other family members. Pre-school children also have access to tablets outside of the home, mainly at the homes of grandparents, other family members and friends.

Marsh et al. (2015) also discovered that there are age and gender differences across many aspects of tablet use. Older children are more likely to own their own tablets, as are boys: 27% of boys and 24% of girls aged under three own their own tablets compared to 40% of boys and 32% of girls aged 3–5. Children aged 3–5 are more likely to use educational apps, such as style creation, obstacles, basic strategy or virtual world creation than their younger counterparts. They enjoy using apps across a range of genres, their favourite ones allowing them to watch videos, listen to music, play games, draw and paint, create virtual worlds, look after pets, dress up avatars and engage in role play. On a typical day, young children use tablets for 1 hour 19 minutes and on a typical weekend day for 1 hour 23 minutes, with the peak period being 4 pm and 6 pm. Their use of tablets in the living room is sometimes linked to non-digital, related items such as dolls and soft toys and they like apps that relate to television, films and iconic characters. Much of the use of this digital technology can be seen as creative and playful because it offers opportunities for young children to engage as producers (Bruns, 2006), re-mixing and mashing-up cultural content in the production of new texts (Lankshear and Knobel, 2006).

Another large-scale survey by Marsh et al. (2005) explored young children's use of popular culture, media and new technologies in 10 local authorities in England. They concluded that many young children, aged from birth to six, were competent users of technologies from an early age and that parents felt that their children had developed a wide range of skills, knowledge and understanding in their use. A similar study by Plowman et al. (2010) surveyed 346 families in Scotland and carried out 24 case studies of young children's use of technology in the home. They discovered that children and parents were active users of technology, but patterns of interaction varied across families due to such factors as parental experience. With media and digital cultures now at the centre of leisure consumption for young children, there have been growing concerns about the sexualisation and commercialisation of childhood.

Commercialisation and Sexualisation of Childhood

Over the last two centuries Anglophone culture has been engrossed by the innocent, endangered child and its pathologised counterpart, the erotic or sexually knowing child.

Both images operate as an indicator of social decay or progress, a signal of impending societal doom or as a utopian possibility for reshaping the future (Renold et al., 2015).

Increasingly perceived as consumers and objects of desire, young children are targets of commercial advertising from a very young age, earlier than in previous generations (Ekström, 2007). This process of mass consumption starts well before birth: according to Cook (2008: 236) we need to question the assumption that 'posits children as somehow outside the realm of economic life who are then brought into it either by caring adults, like parents or teachers, or dragged in by media and marketers'.

In contemporary times the 'child consumer' is therefore made well before it is born. Cook (2008) argues that childhood as a social institution precedes any individual child and that commercial interests and parental/caretaker considerations influence the imagining of the child prior to birth and biographical social existence. Mothers, fathers, partners, relatives and friends anticipate children in their own ways, ahead of any moment of an actual birth, often using commercial products to help visualise and make material the not-yet existing person. Giving gifts to the not-yet born often occurs during the ritual of the baby shower, as well as informally by prospective aunts, grandmothers and friends of the mother-to-be (Clarke, 2004). Parents regularly name the child before birth or adoption and some put significant time, thought and money into decorating a child's room before its arrival.

Practices like these assist in prospectively defining a space ahead of any particular child, one that it can inhabit culturally as well as physically. For Cook (2008) the recognition of the active presence of the anticipated child – whether it occurs in the lives of families or in the planning sessions of marketing agencies – is a key analytic move in the study of consumer culture because it separates the notion of 'consumer' from its simple economic contexts and individualistic assumptions. He argues that by acknowledging children both as economic actors and significant objects for consumption we can bring women, mothers and caretakers into our analysis. When young children are viewed as social-economic actors who are dependent in various ways on the actions of caretakers, the relational and co-productive nature of acquiring, having and displaying products becomes evident and unavoidable. As dependent beings, they rely on adults – usually, but not exclusively, on mothers – for most of everything in their lives. It is largely mothers' work that provides for them, materially, socially and emotionally. Much caring work gets accomplished through the marketplace in the purchasing, preparing, gifting and provisioning of goods and services (see England and Folbre, 2005; Hochschild, 2005), often without the knowledge, request or assent of young children.

Commercial products are particularly targeted at young girls whose sexualised images encourage girls to 'grow up too fast' and become 'too sexy too soon' (Vares and Jackson, 2010). This increased sexualisation of culture also includes the eroticised content of music videos; the marketing of clothing and accessories that sell or represent sexualised identities (for example clothes bearing slogans such as 'porn star' or 'fcuk me' or young children's toys and accessories adorned with the Playboy bunny) (Gill et al., 2010). Take, for example, the doll Barbie, which has been a popular item with girls since its introduction over 50 years ago. It is now linked with a range of commercial items, such as toys, books, games, videos, music, clothing, kitchenware, furniture and foodstuffs. Marsh (2010) interviewed 5–8-year-old children playing in two virtual worlds, Club Penguin and Barbie Girls, where users can earn coins by playing games and spend these coins dressing their avatars and 'homes'. Both virtual worlds offer free membership but also an additional layer of paid membership which provides access to extra goods and in-world opportunities. She suggests that these child-orientated digital worlds of consumption can be explained by the development of social, economic and cultural capital (see Chapter 4 where I discussed Bourdieu and the emergence of a distinctive social habitus for young children): young children who have more economic capital can afford to buy membership which enables them to acquire more cultural goods in the virtual worlds, developing extensive social networks with other paid members in exclusive, 'members-only' events.

Martens et al. (2004) similarly suggest that an application of a Bourdieusian approach is important for revealing the role that consumption plays in the social construction of 'childhood' and 'adulthood'. Young children can act as symbolic representations of their parents' cultural orientations and attitudes: Bourdieu's (1999) ethnographic accounts of the French working class detail fathers' hopes and expectations that their children would inherit their cultural orientations and that their children's acceptance of them reflected and displayed the legitimacy and merit of such orientations. Although the idea that young children reflect their parents' material and social status may seem an obvious point, it highlights the relationality between parents and children when we are thinking about distinctive patterns of consumption.

Accounts of children's consumption have tended to focus on older children, with limited attention being paid to social context: the type of questions that ought to interest the researcher should be different from those appropriate in households with older children. For Martens et al. (2004), the key issue is how capital is transferred between generations and through what processes the habitus becomes internalised. Other related questions concern how and from whom/where children learn to consume; how skills related to competent practice, cultural values and the formation of taste are transmitted between generations; how ideological notions of consumer autonomy and citizenship might be generated in children's consumption; and the types of distinction that parents can 'achieve' through their children.

Martens et al. (2004) argue that the parent–child relationship should take centre stage in accounts of why children consume the way that they do. Parents' habitus (as constrained by their capital) will determine the cultural values employed to raise their children and the internalisation of those values will act to represent their parents' habitus while, at the same time, shaping their own. For example, parents provide economic capital (which may prove important in gaining access to social networks), but, as children grow older, it may well be their social capital (their friends, family, parents' friends and institutional contacts such as schools) that most influences their consumption. In such cases, how cultural capital is accumulated is not simply a process of transfer between parents and young children, but between a range of social networks and institutional relationships. Young children's consumption is therefore related to a set of complex interrelationships, only some of which can be associated with mechanisms of familial distinction.

In the twentieth-first century this commercialisation of childhood is intimately connected with a concern about the sexualisation of young children, where sexualisation is understood not only in relation to young children's self-concept but to how *adults view* young children (Faulkner, 2010). 'Sexuality' has come to be conceived as a most private and integral aspect of a human being. Similarly, childhood is understood as holding the secret to the self, humanity's innermost innocent nature, to which adults have access only by means of their children. Depictions in magazines and on television of young children adopting 'coquettish' postures, the wearing of make-up or adult-looking clothes and the products marketed to children are all identified as signs of the decline of childhood innocence. Today the greatest risk to young children is apparently posed by the paedophile, fuelled by a mass media that constructs children as innocent victims of adult desire and sexuality (Kincaid, 1998).

Danielle Egan and Gail Hawkes (2007, 2008; Hawkes and Egan, 2008) have traced the history of concerns about childhood sexualisation in campaigns around 'child purity' in the late nineteenth century and in the childrearing manuals of the 1930s and 1940s from England, Australia and the USA. They concluded that there was both a progressive and restrictive new discourse that normalised the 'sexual child' but insisted on the need for expert guidance in its management in order to produce 'stable' adults. They argue that such campaigns reflected a strange ambivalence about childhood sexuality: innocent yet seen as a potentially unstoppable force once it becomes corrupted.

Young Children's Sexuality

As part of a scientifically orientated exploration that took place at the end of the nineteenth and during the early part of the twentieth century (Garton, 2003; Weeks, 2003), young children's sexuality was understood by many experts from different disciplines as part of a child's 'normal' development (Egan and Hawkes, 2008). The work of Sigmund Freud is the most famous in this area and he has been commonly credited with discovering childhood sexuality, though his ideas on the topic emerged within a particularly prolific moment in the history of childhood sexuality when many of his less well-known contemporaries such as Havelock Ellis (1915) and Albert Moll (1912) had similar concerns. In his *Three Essays on Sexuality* Freud (2000 [1905]) criticised the Victorian fixation on innocence which pathologised the sexual feelings and activities of young children.

What made Freud's thinking so radical was his acknowledgement and detailed discussion of the young child's sexuality – in his theory of infantile sexuality the child is born with a range of instincts that direct the child's interaction with its own body. His theory was so 'outrageous' (Gittins, 1998) because he gave back to young children their sexuality, defined in term of corporeal experience – they experience sexual pleasure throughout their bodies and various orifices. The pleasures a baby experiences come from many different sources: from being fed or held, from playing with its feet or fingers, from having its nappy changed or moving its bowels, and from being tickled or sung to. Although these early pleasures are not sex-specific or based on who performs them, they lie at the root of all our later sensual and sexual development.

However, we should also not forget the rich British psychoanalytical tradition that stemmed from the work of Melanie Klein and her immediate group of fellow psychoanalysts such as Wilfred Bion and Donald Winnicott (Shuttleworth, 1989). Some of this important research continues today through the Tavistock Clinic in London and in recent work that argues that key psychoanalytical concepts may be useful for understanding emotional relationships in nursery settings (see Elfer, 2007). Within this tradition, Adam Phillips (1998) is an important psychoanalytic thinker, able to shed new light on the Freudian legacy by reinterpreting why young children become so interested in learning and knowing about sexuality. He argues that psychoanalysis has mislaid the young child who has an astonishing capacity for pleasure, a feeling which often unsettles adults who euphemistically refer to it as 'affection': 'This child who can be deranged by hope and anticipation – by an ice-cream – seems to have a passionate love of life, a curiosity of life that for some reason isn't always easy to sustain' (1998: 21).

Even today there is still a great deal of 'resistance' in recognising the important contribution of psychoanalytical approaches in early childhood, partly because adults (academics and early years professionals) find it extremely difficult to overcome barriers of shame and embarrassment when discussing the sexuality of young children. Elias (2012: 164) argues that when young children necessarily encroach again and again on the adult threshold of repugnance, they 'cross the adult shame frontier and penetrate emotional danger zones which the adults themselves can only control with difficulty'. When a child's desires directly contradict adult constructions their manifestation is blamed on 'others' who are deemed to be the cause of such 'dangerous' incitements. Such attempts to control young children's sexuality have produced a paradoxical logic which clings to the asexual child while simultaneously creating various techniques to regulate his or her sexuality (Egan and Hawkes, 2008). By separating young children from the adult sphere of life and denying them participation in the discourses through which we understand sexuality, adults make them even more vulnerable to the desires of others, stripping them of any defences upon which the more experienced child might draw (Egan and Hawkes, 2007).

The voices of young children themselves and how they make sense of their own lives are also conspicuously absent from historical and contemporary discourses on childhood sexuality. In an evaluation of the research evidence on the impact of 'sexualised' media and products on children, Buckingham (2009: 26) writes that 'almost all of the research on the impact of these developments relates to adults rather than children; and, insofar as it addresses children at all, to girls rather than boys'. More often than not, adult preoccupations and anxieties about the corruption of young children's sexuality dominate government-commissioned reviews and reports, potentially damaging their rights to sexual self-expression and agency (Bragg, 2012). There is a refusal to recognise that young children's claims to pleasure and knowledge are an important part of sexual agency; 'the idea that a child has the right to claim its body, pleasure and knowledge would be as abhorrent now as it was historically' (Egan and Hawkes, 2008: 364).

The extent to which the sexuality of young children is marginalised clearly emerges during discussions of sexual rights and the way that they are often interpreted in very narrow terms. Children's rights as sexual subjects are often framed as the right of protection from sexual exploitation, but rarely do adults consider the equally important right of sexual agency (Lehr, 2008). Young children's access to sexual knowledge has usually been considered too 'risky' and controversial due to the fraught relationship between childhood and sexuality. Working with young children aged three to five and their parents, Davies and Robinson (2010) explored the relationship between risk and regulation associated with providing children with accurate knowledge about sexuality. Two main issues were examined: parents' anxieties associated with educating their children about sexuality; and how children actively build narratives around relationships and sexual knowledge based on the fragments of information available to them. Their research indicated that children at young ages constitute their own narratives about gender, relationships and sexuality from various sources – with their peers they collaboratively fill in their knowledge gaps, with dominant children often regulating which knowledge is accepted by the group.

Davies and Robinson (2010) also examined the tensions that exist for parents around the discourse of child protection and the ways in which this influences the education of young children about sexual matters. They discovered that the dominant discourses of childhood innocence constructed from parental interviews often negate the effective education of young children around sexuality, gender and ethical relationships. Sexual knowledge for young children is regularly constituted within the framework of sexual abuse and notions of danger, rather than knowledge that might make a significant contribution to their competency. This anxiety is reinforced through official child protection documents in which knowledge about sexuality is constituted as a key indicator in determining the potential of a young child having experienced sexual abuse.

Conclusions

This chapter has discussed how new media technologies have become an important part of young children's lives in today's society. Through their negotiations around such technologies, young children define themselves as consumers and gendered subjects (Walkerdine, 2009). Walkerdine (2007), for example, has adopted a relational approach to understanding children's engagements with video games. She argues that these games should be seen as sites for the performance of well-regulated femininities and masculinities, where girls are ambivalently positioned in game playing: they must simultaneously be competitive and cooperative. Although competence in games increases boys' status amongst other boys, for girls it mitigates against their friendships with other girls. The boys playing video games are encouraged to achieve success and curb aggression, while girls are subtly regulated against game playing.

Although intense feelings of competition and anxiety occur over the access and consumption of these technologies, I argued that by focusing on moral panics we can be led away from some of the deeper roots upon which they are largely based – the fear of childhood sexuality. Since the nineteenth century there have been continuing public debates about the sexualisation of childhood, with competing explanations offered by professionals on how best to understand young children's sexual experiences. Two important implications stem from our historical analysis that are relevant to contemporary debates. First, concerns about how to manage the 'normal' sexuality of young children without sexualising them are far from new. The frequency with which various reform movements have emerged in the last two centuries indicates that the 'problem' of childhood sexuality has never been adequately resolved. Second, young children's agency has often been marginalised in child-rearing manuals that were more concerned with adults' perceptions of the sexuality of young children and how to manage and control it. In the dominant discourse of childhood the 'innocence' of young children that is so tenaciously protected by adults can often lead to an increase in their vulnerability (Kitzinger, 1990).

However, in any discussion of young children's sexual behaviour, it is important to consider their education about relationships so that they may become competent, ethical sexual citizens. An important way of developing young children's resilience is to provide them with suitable opportunities to learn about sexuality and ethical sexual relationships. Sex education in the early years can lead to more responsible behaviour in intimate relationships and rarely, if ever, leads to early sexual initiation (UNESCO, 2009). Britzman's (1998) work is of particular importance here because she emphasises the troublesome process of reconceptualising education around sexuality. Her examination of affect in pedagogy focuses on learning in terms of what she calls, 'difficult knowledge', which 'is felt as interference or as critique of the self's coherence or view of itself in the world' (Britzman, 1998: 118). Sexuality is not just knowledge that adults find problematic and uncomfortable, but is based upon relations of power between adults and young children that are maintained and reproduced within society. The strict regulation of young children's knowledge of sexuality maintains definitions of the 'child' and 'adult' within and across these categories. In the next chapter we will draw some important conclusions on how such a relational understanding of childhood and adulthood can help us develop a critical sociology of early childhood.

DISCUSSION ACTIVITY

Watch this video on YouTube:

www.youtube.com/watch?v=FGAWSCb8GhU&feature=youtube_gdata_player

1. Why do you think this song was used for a car advert on television?

2. Listen carefully to the lyrics, which were originally written by a group called The Free Design. What type of childhood is being evoked?

3. In contemporary society, should children be given more opportunities to be 'young and free'?

Further Reading

Lydia Plowman and Joanna McPake (2013) 'Seven Myths about Young Children and Technology', *Childhood Education*, 89(1): 27-33.

This discussion of the seven 'myths' is based on detailed case studies with more than 50 three- and four-year-old children and their families, providing rich detail about how and why media technologies are used. All of the children in the studies attended pre-school in central Scotland, typically for a half-day session, with a minority of the children attending for a full working day. Plowman and McPake identified a number of areas for consideration by early years educators which can be summarised as the need to:

- Recognise young children's different preferences
- Develop an awareness of the role of a wide range of technologies in the child's home learning environment
- Acknowledge the range and diversity of children's early experiences at home and the ways in which parents, siblings and caregivers induct children into culturally significant technological practices
- Extend their vision of the nature of young children's technological competences beyond operational skills.

Jackie Marsh (2006) 'Emergent Media Literacy: Digital Animation in Early Childhood', *Language and Education*, 20(6): 493–506.

In this paper Jackie Marsh, one of the foremost scholars in young children's use of new media technologies, outlines a research project in which three- and four-year-old children in one nursery engaged with editing software to create short animated films, some of which were planned initially using storyboards. Animated films are created by sequencing a series of still images until they give the appearance of movement. They can be produced in various ways – through drawings, models and computer graphics – and they form a large part of many children's cultural pleasures. She argues that greater attention should be paid to media education in early childhood by governments and policy makers who are responsible for the development of the early childhood curriculum.

Joanne Faulkner (2011) *The Importance of Being Innocent: Why We Worry about Children*. Cambridge: Cambridge University Press.

An accessible and thought-provoking book that addresses the current debate about the sexualisation of children, predation on them by pae-dophiles and the risks posed to their 'innate innocence' by perceived problems and threats in contemporary society. Joanne Faulkner argues that, contrary to popular opinion, social issues have been sensationalised in moral panics about children who are often presented as neglected, abused, medicated and driven to anti-social behaviour by television and computers. She argues that modern Western society has reacted to prob-lems plaguing the adult world by fetishising children as innocents who must be protected from social realities.

References

Adams, M. (1950) 'Programmes for the Young Viewer', *BBC Quarterly*, 5(9): 81–89.

Astroff, R. and Nyberg, A.K. (1992) 'Discursive Hierarchies and the Construction of Crisis in the News: A Case Study', *Discourse and Society*, 3(1): 5–24.

Australian Senate (2008) *Sexualisation of Children in Contemporary Media.* Parliament of Australia. Available at: www.aph.gov.au/binaries/senate/com mittee/eca_ctte/sexualisation_of_children/report/report.pdf

BBC/ITA (1960) *Children and Television Programmes* (O'Conor Report). London: BBC/ITA.

Bourdieu, P. (1999) *The Weight of the World: Social Suffering in Contemporary Society.* Cambridge: Polity Press.

Bragg, S. (2012) 'Dockside Tarts and Modesty Boards: A Review of Recent Policy on Sexualisation', *Children and Society*, 26: 406–414.

Britzman, D. (1998) *Lost Subjects, Contested Objects: Toward a Psychoanalytic Inquiry of Learning.* New York: State University of New York Press.

Broadcasting Act (1990) London: HMSO.

Bruns, A. (2006) 'Towards Produsage: Futures for User-led Content Production', in F. Sudweeks, H. Hrachovec and C. Ess (eds), *Proceedings: Cultural Attitudes towards Communication and Technology.* Perth: Murdoch University, pp. 275–284.

Buckingham, D. (2005) *The Media Literacy of Children and Young People.* London: Ofcom Report.

Buckingham, D. (2009) *The Impact of the Commercial World on Children's Wellbeing: Report of an Independent Assessment.* London: DCSF/DCMS.

Buckingham, D. and Bragg, S. (2004) *Young People, Sex and the Media: The Facts of Life?* London: Palgrave.

Buckingham, D. and Jensen, H.S. (2012) 'Beyond Media Panics', *Journal of Children and Media*, 6(4): 413–429.

Buckingham, D., Davies, H., Jones, K. and Kelley, P. (1999) *Children's Television in Britain: History, Discourse and Policy.* London: British Film Institute.

Childwise (2014) 'The Monitor Pre-School Report 2014: Key Behaviour Patterns among 0–4 Year Olds'. Available at: www.childwise.co.uk

Clarke, A. (2004) 'Maternity and Materiality: Becoming a Mother in Consumer Culture', in J. Taylor, L. Layne and D. Wozniak (eds), *Consuming Motherhood.* New Brunswick: Rutgers University Press, pp. 55–71.

Communications Act (2003). London: HMSO.

Cook, D. (2008) 'The Missing Child in Consumption Theory', *Journal of Consumer Culture*, 8(2): 219–243.

Critcher, C. (2008) 'Making Waves: Historical Aspects of Public Debates about Children and Mass Media', in S. Livingstone and K. Drotner (eds), *International Handbook of Children, Media and Culture.* London: Sage, pp. 91–104.

Davies, C. and Robinson, K.H. (2010) 'Hatching Babies and Stork Deliveries: Constructing Sexual Knowledge and Taking Risks in Early Childhood Education', *Contemporary Issues in Early Childhood. Special Issue, Risky Childhoods*, 11(3): 249–262.

Davies, M.M. (2010) *Children, Media and Culture*. Maidenhead: Open University Press.

Department for Education (DfE) (2011) *Letting Children be Children: Report of an Independent Review of the Commercialisation and Sexualisation of Childhood*. London: Department for Education.

Egan, R.D. and Hawkes, G.L. (2007) 'Producing the Prurient through the Pedagogy of Purity: Childhood Sexuality and the Social Purity Movement', *Journal of Historical Sociology*, 20(4): 443–461.

Egan, R.D. and Hawkes, G.L. (2008) 'Imperiled and Perilous: Exploring the History of Childhood Sexuality', *Journal of Historical Sociology*, 21(4): 355–367.

Egan, R.D. and Hawkes, G.L. (2010) *Theorizing the Sexual Child in Modernity*. London: Palgrave Macmillan.

Ekström, K. (2007) 'Parental Consumer Learning or "Keeping up with the Children"', *Journal of Consumer Behaviour*, 6(4): 203–217.

Elfer, P. (2007) 'Babies and Young Children in Nurseries: Using Psycho-analytic Ideas to Explore Tasks and Interactions', *Children and Society*, 21(2): 111–122.

Elias, N. (2012) *On the Process of Civilisation*. Dublin: University College Press [Collected Works, vol. 3].

Ellis, H. (1915) *Studies in the Psychology of Sex. Vol. II: Sexual Inversion*. New York: Emerson Books.

England, P. and Folbre, N. (2005) 'Gender and Economic Sociology', in N. Smelser and R. Swedberg (eds), *Handbook of Economic Sociology*, 2nd edition. Princeton, NJ: Princeton University Press, pp. 627–649.

Erasmus, D. (1965 [1655]) *The Colloquies of Erasmus*. Chicago: Chicago University Press.

Faulkner, J. (2010) 'The Innocence Fetish: The Commodification and Sexualisation of Children in the Media and Popular Culture', *Media International Australia*, 135(1): 106–117.

Freud, S. (2000 [1905]) *Three Essays on Sexuality*. New York: Basic Books.

Garton, S. (2003) *Histories of Sexuality Antiquity to Sexual Revolution*. New York: Routledge.

Gill, R., Renold, E. and Ringrose, J. (2010) *Pornified? Complicating the Debates about the Sexualisation of Culture*. An ESRC-funded seminar series.

Gittins, D. (1998) *The Child in Question*. London: Macmillan.

Hawkes, G.L. and Egan, D.R. (2008) 'Developing the Sexual Child', *Journal of Historical Sociology*, 21(4): 443–465.

Himmelweit, H.T., Oppenheim, A.N. and Vince, P. (1958) *Television and the Child*. Oxford: Oxford University Press.

Hochschild, A. (2005) '"Rent-a-Mom" and Other Services: Markets, Meanings and Emotions', *International Journal of Work Organization and Emotion*, 1(1): 74–86.

Holloway, D., Green, L. and Livingstone, S. (2013) *Zero to Eight: Young Children and their Internet Use*. London: EU Kids Online. Available at: http://eprints.lse.ac.uk/52630/

Jackson, S. (1982) *Childhood Sexuality*. London: Blackwell Press.

Kincaid, J.R. (1998) *Erotic Innocence: The Culture of Child Molesting*. Durham, NC: Duke University Press.

Kitzinger, J. (1990) 'Who are You Kidding? Children, Power and the Struggle against Sexual Abuse', in A. James and A. Prout (eds), *Constructing and Reconstructing Childhood: Contemporary Issues in the Sociological Study of Childhood*. London: The Falmer Press, pp. 157–183.

Lankshear, C. and Knobel, M. (2006) *New Literacies: Everyday Practices and Classroom Learning*, 2nd edition. Maidenhead: Open University Press.

Lehr, V. (2008) 'Developing Sexual Agency: Rethinking Late Nineteenth and Early Twentieth Century Theories for the Twenty-First Century', *Sexuality and Culture*, 12(4): 204–220.

Livingstone, S., Haddon, L., Görzig, A. and Ólafsson, K. (2011) *Risks and Safety on the Internet: The UK Report*. LSE, London: EU Kids Online.

Marsh, J. (2010) 'Young Children's Play in Online Virtual Worlds', *Journal of Early Childhood Research*, 8(1): 23–39.

Marsh, J. and Bishop, J.C. (2014) *Changing Play: Play, Media and Commercial Culture from the 1950s to the Present Day*. Buckingham: Open University Press.

Marsh, J., Brooks, G., Hughes, J., Ritchie, L., Roberts, S. and Wright, K. (2005) *Digital Beginnings: Young Children's Use of Popular Culture, Media and New Technologies*. Sheffield: University of Sheffield.

Marsh, J., Plowman, L., Yamada-Rice, D., Bishop, J.C., Lahmar, J., Scott, F., Davenport, A., Davis, S., French, K., Piras, M., Thornhill, S., Robinson, P. and Winter, P. (2015) 'Exploring Play and Creativity in Pre-Schoolers' Use of Apps: Final Project Report'. Available at: http://techandplay.org/tap-media-pack.pdf

Martens, L., Scott, S. and Southerton, D. (2004) 'Bringing Children (and Parents) into the Sociology of Consumption', *Journal of Consumer Culture*, 4(2): 155–182.

Moll, A. (1912) *The Sexual Life of the Child*. London: Macmillan.

Ofcom (2014) *Children and Parents: Media Use and Attitudes Report*. Available at: http://stakeholders.ofcom.org.uk/market-data-research/other/research-publications/childrens/children-parents-oct-14/

Ofcom (2015) *Children and Parents: Media Use and Attitudes Report*. Available at: http://stakeholders.ofcom.org.uk/market-data-research/other/research-publications/childrens/children-parents-nov-15/

Ofcom Broadcasting Code (2015) London: Ofcom.

Ofcom Guidance Notes (2015) 'Section One: Protecting the Under 18s'. Available at: http://stakeholders.ofcom.org.uk/broadcasting/guidance/programme-guidance/bguidance/

Ólafsson, K., Livingstone, S. and Haddon, L. (2013) *Children's Use of Online Technologies in Europe: A Review of the European Evidence Base*. LSE, London: EU Kids Online.

Oswell, D. (1995) 'Watching with Mother in the 1950s', in C. Bazalgette and D. Buckingham (eds), *In Front of the Children: Screen Entertainment and Young Audiences*. London: British Film Institute, pp. 34–46.

Palmer, S. (2006) *Toxic Childhood: How the Modern World is Damaging Our Children and What We Can Do About It*. London: Orion.

Papadopoulos, L. (2010) *Sexualisation of Young People: Review*. London: DfEE.

Phillips, A. (1998) *The Beast in the Nursery*. London: Faber and Faber.

Pilkington Committee (1962) *Report of the Committee on Broadcasting*. London: HMSO.

Plowman, L., McPake, J. and Stephen, C. (2010) 'The Technologisation of Childhood? Young Children and Technology in the Home', *Children and Society*, 24(1): 63–74.

Plummer, K. (1995) *Telling Sexual Stories: Power, Intimacy and Social Worlds*. London: Routledge.

Postman, N. (1994) *The Disappearance of Childhood*. New York: Vintage.

Renold, E., Ringrose, J. and Egan, R.D. (2015) 'Introduction', in E. Renold, J. Ringrose and D.R. Egan (eds), *Children, Sexuality and Sexualization*. London: Palgrave Macmillan, pp. 1–20.

Robinson, K.H. (2012) '"Difficult Citizenship": The Precarious Relationships between Childhood, Sexuality and Access to Knowledge', *Sexualities*, 15(3/4): 257–276.

Robinson, K.H. and Jones Diaz, C. (2006) *Diversity and Difference in Early Childhood: Issues for Theory and Practice*. Maidenhead: Open University Press.

Rohloff, A. and Wright, S. (2010) 'Moral Panic and Social Theory: Beyond the Heuristic', *Current Sociology*, 58(3): 403–419.

Rush, E. and la Nauze, A. (2006) *Corporate Paedophilia, Sexualisation of Children in Australia*, Discussion Paper Number 90, Australian National University: The Australia Institute.

Shuler, C. (2012) *iLearn II: An Analysis of the Education Category of Apple's App Store*. Available at: www.joanganzcooneycenter.org/wpcontent/uploads/2012/01/ilearnii.pdf

Shuttleworth, J. (1989) 'Psychoanalytic Theory and Infant Development', in L. Miller, M. Rustin, M. Rustin and J. Shuttleworth (eds), *Closely Observed Infants*. London: Duckworth, pp. 22–51.

UNESCO (2009) *International Technical Guidance in Sexuality Education: An Evidence-informed Approach for Schools, Teachers and Health Educators*. Paris: UNESCO.

Vares, T. and Jackson, S. (2010) 'Preteen Girls Read "Tween" Popular Culture: A Contribution to the "Sexualisation of Girlhood" Debates'. Paper presented at Child and Teen Consumption Conference, Linkoping, Sweden, June.

Walkerdine, V. (2007) *Children, Gender and Video Games: Towards a Relational Approach to Multimedia*. Basingstoke: Palgrave Macmillan.

Walkerdine, V. (2009) 'Developmental Psychology and the Study of Childhood', in M.J. Kehilly (ed.), *An Introduction to Childhood Studies*, 2nd edition. Maidenhead: Open University Press/McGraw Hill, pp. 112–123.

Weeks, J. (2003) *Sexuality*, 2nd edition. London: Routledge.

8

CONCLUSIONS

This book has argued that there is an urgent need to develop a relational sociology of early childhood, one that focuses on the earliest experiences of young children. Young children are born into interdependent relationships that existed before them: as they grow up these relationships with their parents, siblings and friends change but are structured by different societies and in different historical epochs. One of the key arguments in this book is that in order to develop a distinctive sociology of early childhood, one should not only focus on the relational aspects of early childhood and adulthood, but also at the same time view them as long-term processes with deep historical roots. In Chapter 2, I explained how these social processes should be seen as dynamic and structured - although transitions occur in dramatic spurts, the history of childhood does not proceed in discrete stages. Short-term changes must be both distinguished from and connected to underlying developments in the long run.

Pierre Bourdieu and Norbert Elias, two of the most eminent relational sociologists, have been used to explain how adults use their positions of power to define and maintain differences between adults and young children. Although Bourdieu mainly focused on school-age children and adults, his concepts can easily be adapted to study the lives of infants, toddlers and pre-school children, as well as those just entering school. His theoretical framework is important for providing a set of relational conceptual tools – capital, habitus and field – that can be finely tuned to explain the shifting fields of power that affect the lives of young children in changing institutions.

In a recent book entitled *Childhood with Bourdieu* there are four chapters that apply his theoretical perspective to early childhood (Alanen et al., 2015), reflecting a growing interest in the way that sociologists of childhood can apply this perspective to understanding young children's lives. One of them, by Pascale Garnier, is particularly insightful – she uses Bourdieu to explain the contribution of parents to the educational progress of pre-school children in the French *école maternelle*, emphasising the tension between educational strategies and a practical family life where some parents felt the need to preserve it from academic pressure. Garnier (2015) argues that during the nursery years, situated practices can take into account the child as 'being' as well as 'becoming' and invites us to rethink the concept of age. The 'age' of children should not be considered a difficulty for sociological analysis; rather 'studying practices opens the doors to a sociological analysis of the different ages of children' (Garnier, 2015: 73).

Age remains one of the most contentious categories that haunt previous and recent attempts to develop a new sociology of childhood, mainly due to its close associations with the developmental model of childhood. It is such a contentious issue because it draws attention to some of the unresolved tensions in the relationship between *natural* or biological processes and the *social*. A good example is the article by James (2010), a bold attempt to overcome competing theoretical perspectives based on the dichotomy between one universal category of childhood and multiple childhoods. In developing his argument, other dichotomies, like the adult–child one, keep emerging and encouraging him to take a closer look at age differences between children and young people. Although James mentions that the English language contains important relational terms to distinguish between different aspects of childhood - a newborn, an infant, a babe-in-arms, a toddler, a child - he remains steadfast in his rejection of 'a hegemonic developmental perspective' (James, 2010: 490).

Morrow (2013: 154) similarly remarks that although being an infant or a young person is important, underlying assumptions about age 'run the risk of solidifying developmental thinking', limiting the relational child to a specific chronological age group. However Uprichard (2008) offers an alternative perspective by arguing that childhood is a stage of the human life course that chronologically precedes adulthood, part of a biological and irreversible ageing process: 'being' a child *and* 'becoming' an adult is necessarily bound by the 'arrow of time' (Coveney and Highfield, 1990). Uprichard attempts to uncover some of the temporal dimensions that lie behind the 'being' and 'becoming' discourses in different constructions of childhood: children are not only aware that older people were once younger, or that they will change as they become older, but they also have different views and experiences about what it means to age in a changing world. The children in her interviews negotiated and imagined their future lives – they were constructing themselves as 'being and becomings'. Mona, a five-year-old living in York, exclaimed, 'I can't wait 'til I'm seven because then I can go to the shops by myself!' In contrast, Sophie, a four-year-old child was not so excited about becoming older because she assumed that being an adult may also be 'boring'.

McNamee and Seymour (2012) again remind us of the central theme in this book – why it is important to distinguish between early childhood and late childhood – by arguing that there is still a lacuna in key 'childhood' journals, making it important to question some of the foundational concepts in the social construction of childhood. They analysed 320 empirical research articles published between 1993 and 2010 in three of the leading journals in childhood studies, *Children and Society*, *Childhood* and *Children's Geographies*, concluding that there was an overemphasis on a particular age group: 10, 11 and 12-year-olds are at least three times as likely to be included as a five-year-old and nearly twice as likely as a 17-year-old. The younger age groups (5–7) were also less likely to be included in the articles than those at the upper end of the childhood continuum, the 15–18-year-olds.

In Chapter 3 I discussed how sociologists of childhood have rejected most forms of 'developmentalism', especially those based on the Piagetian perspective, as a 'stage' and 'age' approach to young children's development. To develop a sociological understanding of young children's lives we need to use a relational approach that will integrate the psychological aspects of children's development, overcoming some of the concerns about the role of developmental psychology. I outlined some of the important connections between Norbert Elias and the well-known Russian developmental psychologist Lev Vygotsky, arguing that both of their theories provide a sophisticated, developmental perspective that can follow the interweaving of biological and social processes as young children learn from their elders how to survive and grow in their societies. We explored how it was possible to build bridges between the individual focus of psychology and the concerns of sociology (Reay, 2015), developing a strong theoretical foundation 'to analyse the genesis of investment in a field of social relations in which the child is increasingly implicated' (Bourdieu, 2000: 166).

To explore in greater depth the social relations of early childhood we discussed important changes in the balance of power between men, women and young children, especially as women have become an integral part of the workforce in developing countries. Men are now expected to become more involved with the care and education of young children. However, a recent report by the Fairness in Families Index (Fatherhood Institute, 2016) found that in the UK parents are officially the worst in the developed world at sharing their childcare responsibilities. The report identifies three key policy changes the UK government could make to hasten progress towards gender equality: redesign parenting leave, moving towards a Scandinavian-style system including a substantial period of well-paid, 'use-it-or-lose-it' leave for fathers; strengthen efforts to reduce the gender pay gap; and require schools and early years, social work and maternity services to publish data on their engagement with fathers, and be inspected by Ofsted and the Care Quality Commission.

Researchers have found that countries with the lowest poverty rates worldwide are those defined by high parental – particularly maternal – employment, as well as low in-work poverty and effective income support policies (OECD, 2007). These countries have generous universal benefits, active employment policies and widely available free or low-cost childcare and service provision. Nevertheless, increased childcare places to encourage mothers back into the workforce pose important dilemmas, as childrearing – including aspects of love and care which might previously have taken place in the family – becomes a complex part of integrated provision. To facilitate such provision, particular staff are responsible for direct work with a small group of children throughout the day and for partnership with these young children's families, a role referred to as the key person approach in the UK (Elfer et al., 2011) or primary caregiver (Weigand, 2007).

Page (2011) suggests that in the context of paid childcare, babies and young children need 'professional love' from their caregivers. She contends that when some mothers recognise reciprocity, they are able to identify attachment as an intellectual experience that is in tune with their own needs for their children, rather than a feeling that is threatening to the mother–child relationship. Noddings' (2003: 24) work on an ethic of care emphasises the importance of reciprocity, namely the giving and receiving of care: young children need close relationships that require the skills of 'stepping out of one's own personal frame of reference and into the other's'. When professional carers can make this shift in their thinking, they are able to support babies and young children.

For McCarthy and Prokhovnik (2014) the key insight of relational approaches such as the ethic of care is that the individual is not self-contained but operates at both material and symbolic levels with a self-understanding which builds from and continues to function in relation to others. They argue that feminist theorising of care emphasises personal and embodied relational connections rather than abstract principles (Philip et al., 2012). From this grounded perspective, care encompasses embodied labour and love, caring for and about, and care receiving. Colley (2006) suggests that in childcare, as in other forms of caring work, the concept of emotional labour helps us to understand how this work is learned and performed. In her case study of a group of childcare students, successful trainees had classed and gendered expectations of a destiny caring for young children: they were not only working upon the emotions of the young children in their care, but on their own feelings in order to learn to labour appropriately.

In Chapter 3 I critically examined some of the underlying assumptions that lie behind Bowlby's theory of attachment, which has been widely accepted or advocated in nursery policy in the UK (DCSF, 2008), in Europe (OECD, 2006), in the USA (Lee, 2006) and in Australia (Ebbeck and Yim, 2009). I argued that this theory is still too narrowly based on the mother or parent and child dyad to capture the relational complexities of young children's social relationships with other significant people in their lives. Elias's important relational concept of love and learning was used as an alternative framework to explore the significance of group processes in young children's relationships, moving beyond the individualistic emphasis given in attachment theory to the parent and child.

Parents, siblings, friends, childcare providers and educators all influence young children's social relationships. What is particularly significant is the role that siblings and peer relationships play in the formation of young children's socio-emotional development. Young children seek, in their peers and friendships, the emotional bonds and feelings of security they first established in families. They value the same dimensions of intimacy, support, trust and mutuality as older children and adults (Dunn, 2004). Passed on from one generation to the next, young children internalise from adults and their peers an enormous social fund of knowledge about the world.

In Chapter 4 we used Bourdieu's concepts of field and internalized dispositions – the social *habitus* of young children – as an important theoretical framework for developing a sociology of early childhood. The social habitus refers to the internalisation of wider structures and processes manifested through the routines and taken-for-granted actions of young children: the longer a young child is located within a particular set of institutional relationships the more likely they are to develop a practical sense of how to behave and act in certain ways. Institutional settings set the tone for the relationships between individual children, dyads (child–caregiver, peer–peer (friendships and playmates)) and group interactions between young children and their caregivers. Within this changing array of people, young children learn about the membership rules of various networks.

As more young children spend their days in nurseries, kindergartens and day centres we need to explain the extent to which they can develop their own social and cultural capital. Play is one very important area where we can observe young children developing their own distinctive stocks of cultural and social capital. As directors of their own play they always strive to have their own separate play culture, and within that, resist against adult power and conventions. Chapter 5 emphasised how radical perspectives on play, such as Bakhtin's concept of the carnival, can be used to illustrate how young children can turn the established adult order on its head, exploring the relational dynamics which shape their relative independence from adults. In a similar way to the carnival, young children try to break down barriers and challenge power inequalities by mocking the hierarchical order set by parents and teachers – they attempt to resist authority and generate disorder to gain more control over their lives.

Benjamin also provides an important way for reconceptualising play by uncovering the different layers of early childhood experience that have become forgotten in adulthood. His writings are an important attempt to restore the earliest impressions of childhood memory which have not yet been tainted by the destructive power of habit. In a 1940s BBC broadcast, *Reminiscences of Childhood*, Dylan Thomas, the famous Welsh poet, provided a good example that illustrates some of the ways we can begin to recover these memories of childhood which 'have no order and no end'. Playing in a modest little park 'full of terrors and treasures', he evokes the many secret places of his childhood: its 'caverns and forests, prairies and deserts, a country somewhere at the end of the sea. … A country just born and always changing' (Thomas, 1943).

In the last two chapters I focused on two crises in contemporary childhood – parenting and the development of new media technologies – arguing that both should be explained through the deep historical roots that connect early childhood and adulthood. These debates are usually driven by passionate feelings about the 'crisis in childhood' occurring in today's society and discussions about the legitimate exercise of professional power. In Chapter 6 I argued that since the eighteenth century some of the major changes in parental advice can be traced to the Romantic vision of the child as 'natural', 'pure' and 'innocent', which was developed by philosophers such as Rousseau to uncover the deeper, more intuitive parts of ourselves concealed under the armour of adulthood. The young child imagined by the Romantics represented a lost childhood 'immune to the pressures of history': isolated and solitary, imaginative and creative, but close to nature and possessed of emotional authority.

According to Elias (2008), these changes in parenting can be explained by a longer trend of informalisation that occurred from the late twentieth century onwards. This trend represents a transition from an authoritarian to a more egalitarian parent–child relationship where there is a loosening of barriers of authority in relations between young children and adults, with young children being given more autonomy and a greater degree of decision making. Although young children have greater autonomy in their relationships with adults, both adults and young children are now expected to exercise a higher degree of self-restraint. One important long-term, unintended consequence is that there are increasing pressures to control and regulate one's emotions and behaviour.

In Chapter 7 I discussed how new media technologies have become an important part of young children's lives in today's society. Although strong feelings of 'public' anxiety occur over the access and consumption of these technologies, I argued that by focusing on moral panics we can be led away from some of the deeper roots upon which they are largely based – the fear of childhood sexuality. Childhood and sexuality share a similar conceptual history from the eighteenth century – I argued that sexuality and sexual knowledge are crucial dimensions in the contemporary Western definition of childhood and adulthood, maintaining boundaries between them and fuelling debates about the moral dangers of new technologies such as the Internet.

The strict regulation of young children's knowledge of sexuality maintains a relational definition of the 'child' and 'adult'. Attempts to regulate young children's sexuality have produced a paradoxical logic which clings to the asexual child while simultaneously creating various techniques to control his or her sexuality (Egan and Hawkes, 2008). By separating young children from the adult sphere of life and denying them participation in the discourses through which they can understand sexuality, adults make young children even more vulnerable to the desires of others. In a letter to his son, Ted Hughes (2007: 513) beautifully captures the vulnerability of the young child and the way that we try to cope with situations that overwhelm our 'inner' childhood:

> So everybody develops a whole armour of secondary self, the artificially constructed being that deals with the outer world, and the crush of circumstances. And when we meet people this is what we usually meet ... But when you develop a strong divining sense for the child behind that armour, and you make your dealings and negotiations only with that child, you find that everybody becomes, in a way, like your own child.

Across generations, in the course of humanity's development we are all connected. For adults and young children, the need to work and think about our relationships never ends. For us this book is the beginning of a long process.

References

Alanen, L., Brooker, L. and Mayall, B. (eds) (2015) *Childhood with Bourdieu*. Basingstoke: Palgrave Macmillan.

Bourdieu, P. (2000) *Pascalian Meditations*. Cambridge: Polity Press.

Colley, H. (2006) 'Learning to Labour with Feeling: Class, Gender and Emotion in Childcare Education and Training', *Contemporary Issues in Early Childhood*, 7(1): 15–29.

Coveney, P. and Highfield, R. (1990) *The Arrow of Time*. London: Flamingo.

Department for Children Schools and Families (DCSF) (2008) *The Early Years Foundation Stage: Setting the Standards for Learning, Development and Care for Children from Birth to Five*. London: DCSF.

Dunn, J. (2004) *Children's Friendships: The Beginnings of Intimacy*. Malden, MA: Blackwell.

Ebbeck, M. and Yim, H. (2009) 'Rethinking Attachment: Fostering Positive Relationships between Infants, Toddlers and their Primary Caregivers', *Early Child Development and Care*, 179(7): 899–909.

Egan, R.D. and Hawkes, G.L. (2008) 'Imperiled and Perilous: Exploring the History of Childhood Sexuality', *Journal of Historical Sociology*, 21(4): 355–367.

Elfer, P., Goldschmied, E. and Selleck, D. (2011) *Key Persons in the Early Years: Building Relationships for Quality Provision in Early Years Settings and Schools*, 2nd edition. London: David Fulton.

Elias, N. (2008) 'The Civilising of Parents', in *Essays II: On Civilising Processes, State Formation and National Identity*. Dublin: UCD Press [The Collected Works, vol. 15], pp. 14–40.

Fatherhood Institute (2016) Fairness in Families Index. Available at: www.father hoodinstitute.org/wp-content/uploads/2016/06/FINALFatherhood-Institute-Capstone-FiFI-2016.pdf

Garnier, P. (2015) 'Between Young Children and Adults: Practical Logic in Families Lives', in L. Alanen, L. Brooker and B. Mayall (eds) *Childhood with Bourdieu*. Basingstoke: Palgrave Macmillan, pp. 57–77.

Hughes, T. (2007) *Letters of Ted Hughes*. London: Faber and Faber.

James, A.L. (2010) 'Competition or Integration? The Next Step in Childhood Studies?', *Childhood*, 17(4): 485–499.

Lee, S. (2006) 'A Journey to a Close, Secure and Synchronous Relationship: Infant–caregiver Relationship Development in a Childcare Context', *Journal of Early Childhood Research*, 4(2): 133–151.

McCarthy, J.R. and Prokhovnik, R. (2014) 'Embodied Relationality and Caring after Death', *Body and Society*, 20(2): 18–43.

McNamee, S. and Seymour, J. (2012) 'Towards a Sociology of 10–12 Year Olds? Emerging Methodological Issues in the "New" Social Studies of Childhood', *Childhood*, 20(2): 156–168.

Morrow, V. (2013) 'What's in a Number? Unsettling the Boundaries of Age', *Childhood*, 20(2): 151–155.

Noddings, N. (2003) *Caring: A Feminine Approach to Ethics and Moral Education*, 2nd edition. Berkeley: University of California Press.

OECD (2006) *Starting Strong II: Early Childhood Education and Care*. Paris: OECD.

OECD (2007) *Babies and Bosses: Reconciling Work and Family Life*. Paris: OECD.

Page, J. (2011) 'Do Mothers Want Professional Carers to Love Their Babies?', *Journal of Early Childhood Research*, 9(3): 310–323.

Philip, G., Rogers, C. and Weller, S. (2012) 'Understanding Care and Thinking with Care', in C. Rogers and S. Weller, *Critical Approaches to Care: Care Relations, Identities and Cultures*. London: Routledge, pp. 1–12.

Reay, D. (2015) 'Habitus and the Psychosocial: Bourdieu with Feelings', *Cambridge Journal of Education*, 45(1): 9–23.

Thomas, D. (1943) *Reminiscences of Childhood*. BBC Radio archives. Available at: www.youtube.com/watch?feature=player_detailpage&v=Ce_qzuBPQpc

Uprichard, E. (2008) 'Children as "Being and Becomings": Children, Childhood and Temporality', *Children and Society*, 22(4): 303–313.

Weigand, R. (2007) 'Reflective Supervision in Childcare: The Discoveries of an Accidental Tourist', *Zero to Three*, pp. 17–22.

INDEX